The Production
of Money

The Production of Money

How to Break the Power of Bankers

ANN PETTIFOR

V E R S O
London • New York

This paperback edition first published by Verso 2018
First published by Verso 2017
© Ann Pettifor 2017, 2018

3 5 7 9 10 8 6 4

Verso
UK: 6 Meard Street, London W1F 0EG
US: 20 Jay Street, Suite 1010, Brooklyn, NY 11201
versobooks.com

Verso is the imprint of New Left Books

ISBN-13: 978 1 78663-135-0
ISBN-13: 978-1-78663-137-4 (US EBK)
ISBN-13: 978-1-78663-136-7 (UK EBK)

British Library Cataloguing in Publication Data
A catalogue record for this book is available from the British Library

The Library of Congress Has Cataloged the Hardback Edition As Follows:

Names: Pettifor, Ann, author.
Title: The production of money : how to break the
power of bankers / Ann
   Pettifor.
Description: Brooklyn, NY : Verso, 2017. | Includes
bibliographical
   references.
Identifiers: LCCN 2016047535| ISBN 9781786631343
(hardback) | ISBN
   9781786631374 (US ebook) | ISBN 9781786631367
(UK ebook)
Subjects: LCSH: Money. | Banks and banking. |
Finance. | Social change. |
   BISAC: BUSINESS & ECONOMICS / Money &
Monetary Policy. | POLITICAL SCIENCE
   / Economic Conditions. | POLITICAL SCIENCE /
Public Policy / Economic
   Policy.
Classification: LCC HG220.A2 .P48 2017 | DDC
332.401—dc23
LC record available at
https://lccn.loc.gov/2016047535

Typeset in Sabon by MJ&N Gavan, Truro, Cornwall
Printed in the UK by CPI Group (UK) Ltd, Croydon
CR0 4YY

Contents

Preface

I wrote a modest little book in the spring of 2006 entitled *The Coming First World Debt Crisis*. It was written as a not-so-subtle warning to friends who had bought into the liberalisation of finance model and were borrowing as if there were no tomorrow. The fear was that because of widespread ignorance about the activities of the global finance sector, and because the economics profession itself did not appear to understand money, banking and debt, ordinary punters were sleepwalking into a crisis.

I did not approve of the publisher's choice for the title, believing that the book would be out of date as soon as it was published in September 2006. By then, surely, the crisis would have come? How wrong I was, and how right the publisher to overrule me. In the meantime I had to submit to some unkind comments on my analysis of the system. In a *Guardian* column written on 29 August 2006, I argued that the previous summer's fall in house sales in Florida and California were canaries in the deep vast coal mine of US sub-prime credit; and that the impact of a credit/debt crisis in the US would have a much greater impact on us all than the then ongoing crisis in Lebanon. 'Chicken-Licken!' the web crowd yelled. Bobdoney – someone I suspect was a City of London trader – waxed lyrical:

> Next week Ann writes about a six-mile-wide asteroid which has just collided with a butterfly in the Van Allen belt and which, even now, as I eat my cucumber sandwich and drink my third cup of tea today, is heading inexorably towards its

final destination just off the coast at Grimsby at 2.30pm on August 29, 2016.

Splosh!

Bobdoney was ten years out, and after the crisis broke, was not heard of again.

The crisis breaks

I remember exactly where I was on that sunny day, 9 August 2007, when it was reported that inter-bank lending had frozen. Bankers knew that their peers were bust, and could not be trusted to honour their obligations. I then naively believed that friends would get the message. I also hoped in vain that the economics profession as a whole would add its voice to those few that warned of catastrophe. Not so. Apart from readers of the *Financial Times*, and of course some speculators in the finance sector itself, very few seemed to notice.

Fully a year later in September 2008 when Lehman Brothers imploded, it dawned on the wider public that the international financial system was broken. By then it was too late. The world was perilously close to complete financial breakdown. The fear that bank customers would not be able to draw cash from ATMs was real. On the Wednesday after Lehman fell, Mohamed El-Erian, CEO of PIMCO, asked his wife to go to the ATM and withdraw as much cash as possible. When she asked why, he said it was because he feared that US banks might not open.[1] Blue-chip industrial companies called the US Treasury to explain they had trouble funding themselves. Over those hair-raising weeks, we lived through a terrifying economic experiment that very nearly did not work.

Given this backdrop, it came as no surprise that policymakers, politicians and commentators had no coherent response to make to the crisis. Many on the left of the political spectrum were just as stunned. Like most economists, they seemed to have a blind spot for the finance sector. Instead their focus was on the economics of the real world: taxation, markets, international trade, the International Monetary Fund (IMF) and World Bank, employment policy, the environment, the public sector. Very few had paid attention to the vast, expanding and intangible activities of the deregulated private finance sector. As a result, very few on the Left (taken as a whole, with clear exceptions), nor the Right for that matter, had a sound analysis of the causes of the crisis, and therefore of the policies that would need to be put in place to regain control over the great public good that is the monetary system.

Bankers, too, were at first stunned into submission, desperate for taxpayer-funded bailouts and, even for a moment, humbled. But that was not to last. After the bailouts, politicians faced a vast policy vacuum. G8 politicians, led by Britain's Gordon Brown, at first co-operated at an international level to stabilise the system. That co-operation and an internationally co-ordinated stimulus quickly evaporated. Worldwide, politicians and policy-makers fell back on, or were once more talked into, orthodox policies for stabilisation, most notably fiscal consolidation. As Naomi Klein had warned, many in the finance sector quickly understood the crisis as an opportunity to reinforce the global financial system's grip on elected governments and markets. After some hesitation they jumped at this opportunity, in contrast to much of the Left, or the social democratic parties.

No fundamental changes were made to the international financial architecture. The Basel Committee on Banking Supervision tinkered with post-crisis reforms, but made no suggestions for structural changes to the international financial architecture and system. Neoliberalism – the dominant economic model – prevailed everywhere. Paul Mason wrote a book in 2009 called *Meltdown* with the subtitle: *The End of the Age of Greed*. How wrong he was. Ten years now from the start of the 2007 recession, while inequality polarizes societies, the world is dominated by an oligopoly greedily accumulating obscene levels of wealth. And despite the initial meltdown, the global financial crisis has not come to an end. Instead it has rolled around from the epicentre of the Anglo-American economies to the Eurozone and is now focused on so-called 'emerging markets'. Private bankers and other financial institutions are gorging on cheap debt issued by central bankers, and have in turn dumped costly debt on firms, households and individuals.

The publics in western economies have suffered the consequences. At the time of writing, millions are in open revolt, backing populist, mostly right-wing political candidates. They hope that these 'strong men and women' will protect them from hard-headed neoliberal policies for unfettered global markets in finance, trade and labour.

The consequences of ongoing financial crises

At a time when a small elite in the finance and tech sectors continue to reap massive financial gains, the International Labour Organisation estimates that worldwide at least 200 million people are unemployed. In some European countries, every second young person is unemployed. The Middle East and North Africa, at the vortex of political, religious and military upheaval, have the highest rate of youth unemployment in the world. Where employment has increased in economies such as Britain's, it is of the insecure, self-employed, part-time, zero-hour-contract kind, with uncertain earnings. Warnings abound of a robotic future and the obsolescence of human labour. This vision is touted as if the supply of minerals essential to robots – including tin, tantalum, tungsten and coltan ore, and the emissions associated with their extraction, are infinite. Yet the failure to provide meaningful work for millions of people – at a time when much needs to be done to transform the economy away from fossil fuels – is barely on the political agenda of most social democratic governments. Few, if any, are calling for full, well-paid and skilled employment.

While global GDP is just $77 trillion, global financial assets have grown to $225 trillion since 2007, according to McKinsey Global Institute. Thanks to unregulated markets in credit, the burden of global debt continues to rise. In 2015 the overhang of debt was at 286 percent of global GDP, compared with 269 percent in 2007.[2] Millions of workers worldwide have gone for seven years without a pay rise. Small and large firms are facing falling prices, followed by falls in profits and bankruptcy. 'Austerity' is crushing the southern economies of Europe, and depressing demand and activity elsewhere. In the United States, nearly one third of all adults, about 76 million people, are either 'struggling to get by' or 'just getting by'.[3]

However, business is better than usual for rentiers – bankers, shadow bankers and other financial institutions that remain upright thanks to taxpayer-backed government guarantees, cheap money and other central banker largesse aimed only at the finance sector. It is also good for the world's new oligopoly – big companies like Apple, Microsoft, Uber and Amazon, making fortunes out of monopolistic, rent-gouging activities.

While these and the top 1 percent of corporations are said to be 'hoarding' cash of about $945 billion, American corporations, as a whole, hold only about $1.84 trillion in cash. These holdings are eclipsed by corporate borrowing. As this goes to press, US corporations have built up $6.6 trillion in debt.[4] In 2015 corporate debt reached three times earnings before interest, taxes, depreciation and amortization – a twelve-year record, according to Bloomberg. In 2015 alone, corporate liabilities jumped by $850 billion, fifty times the increase in cash by Standard & Poor's reckoning. An estimated one third of these companies are unable to generate enough returns on investment to cover the high cost of borrowed money. This poses the risk of bankruptcy for many smaller corporates. Their creditors may be unconcerned, but it is far from improbable that at some point corporate, as opposed to household, debtors could blow up the system, all over again.

There are other canaries in the world's financial 'coal mines' – all warning of another crisis in the globally interconnected financial system. The scariest is deflation: a threat barely understood because so few alive today have ever lived through a deflationary era. Although the threat of deflation is not seriously addressed by politicians and economists, it is now a phenomenon in Europe and Japan, and a threat in China. The latter rescued the global economy in 2009 by launching a massive $600 billion stimulus, which helped keep western economies afloat. Western leaders responded by reverting to orthodox, contractionary policies, thus shrinking demand for China's goods and services. This has left China with an overhang of bank debt, and with gluts of goods like tyres, steel, aluminium and diesel. These gluts drove Chinese producer price inflation below zero for four years before 2016. As this overcapacity was channelled into global markets, so deflationary pressures hit western economies.

Both western politicians and financial commentators welcomed news of falling prices. In May 2015, as the UK officially slipped into deflation for the first time in more than half a century, Britain's Chancellor, George Osborne, welcomed the 'right kind of deflation as good news for families'. He feared 'no damaging cycle of falling prices and wages'.[5] No one in the British political and economic establishment wanted to acknowledge that the fall in prices was a consequence of a slowing world economy and, in particular, of weak demand for labour, finance, goods and services. Instead deflation was dismissed by most mainstream economists as a sign of consumers delaying purchases!

The biggest worry is the effect deflation has on inflating the value of debt and interest rates. As a generalised fall in prices feeds through the global financial system, wages and profits fall, and firms fail. At the same time, inexorably and invisibly, *the value of the stock of debt rises relative to prices and wages*. The cost of debt (the rate of interest) rises too, even while nominal rates may be low, negative or static. Negative *real* interest rates are possible only if *nominal* interest rates are far more negative – and those would be difficult for central bankers to sustain at a political level.

To put it plainly: for an over-indebted global economy, deflation poses a truly frightening threat.

But what concerns me – and many others – is that central bankers have used up the policy tools at their disposal for addressing another globally interconnected financial crisis. In the UK and the US, central bank interest rates were brought down from about 5 percent to near zero after the 2007–09 crisis. Central banks massively expanded their balance sheets by buying up or lending financial and corporate assets (securities) from capital markets, and crediting the accounts of the sellers. In this way the Federal Reserve has added $4.5 trillion to its balance sheet. The Bank of England's balance sheet is bigger, relative to UK gross domestic product, than ever throughout its long history. But while quantitative easing (QE) may have stabilised the financial system, it inflated the value of assets like property – owned on the whole, by the more affluent. As such, QE contributed to rising inequality and to the political and social instability associated with it. So expanding QE further is probably not politically feasible.

Even while monetary policy was loosened, economic recovery stalled or slowed because governments simultaneously tightened fiscal policy. They were encouraged in this strategy of 'austerity' by the mainstream economics profession, central bankers and global institutions such as the IMF and the OECD, all of whom were cheered on by the western media. The result was predictable: the heavily indebted global economy suffered ongoing economic weakness and overlapping recessions. Recovery, especially in Europe, was worse than from the Great Depression of the 1930s, when it took far less time for countries to return to pre-crisis levels of employment, incomes and activity.

As I write, the 'austerity' mood has changed. Global institutions are panic-struck by the volatility of the financial system, by the threats of debt-deflation, a slowing global economy, and by the rise of political populism. In response, by way of extraordinary U-turns, they have radically altered their advice on fiscal consolidation. The IMF, in a May 2016 note, questioned whether neoliberalism had been oversold. The OECD warned policy-makers several times in 2016 to 'act now! To keep promises' – and to expand public spending and investment. In June 2016 the OECD made the sensible case that 'monetary policy alone cannot break out of [the] low-growth trap and may be overburdened. Fiscal space is eased with low interest rates.' Governments were urged to use 'public investment to support growth'.[6] But these new, late converts to fiscal expansion may just as well have banged their heads against a brick wall, for all the listening done by the US Congress and by neoliberal finance ministers such as Germany's Wolfgang Schäuble, Finland's Alexander Stubb, or Britain's George Osborne. The ideology of 'austerity' – aimed at slashing and privatising the public sector – wedded to free market fundamentalism is now so deeply embedded in western government treasuries that tragically neither politicians nor policy-makers are capable of action.

In desperation, some central banks (the European Central Bank and the central banks of Switzerland, Sweden and Japan) have crossed the Rubicon of the Zero Lower Bound, and made interest rates negative. This means lenders pay money to central banks in exchange for the privilege of parking funds (in the form of loans) at the central bank. This is both a sign of a broken monetary system but also of the fear gnawing away at investors, as financial volatility drives them to search for the only 'havens' they now regard as safe for their capital: the debt of sovereign governments.

What is to be done?

So what is to be done by the forces for good – progressive forces – to stabilise the global financial system and restore employment, political stability and social justice?

First, we need wider public understanding of where money comes from and how the financial system operates. Regrettably these are areas of the economy gravely neglected by many progressive and mainstream economists – a convenient blind spot that is no doubt welcome to the finance sector. This new book – *The Production of Money* – is an attempt to simplify key concepts in relation to money, finance and economics, and to make them accessible to a much wider audience, especially to women and environmentalists. It expands on my book *Just Money* (2015) and hopefully adds greater content and clarity to a subject that is not easy to write about. Nevertheless I will persevere, as I am convinced that only wider public understanding of money, credit and the operation of the banking and financial system will lead to significant change.

The second aim of any progressive movement should be to channel the public anger generated by bankers and politicians into a progressive and positive alternative. Sadly, the Right are more effective at channelling public anger into the blaming of immigrants, asylum seekers and other bogeymen. And as worrying, sections of the so-called Left are channelling anger at bankers into neoclassical economic policies for resolving the crisis. Some of these proposals for 'reform' of the banking system are also discussed in this book. They take the form of 'fractional reserve banking', the nationalisation of the money supply and the pursuit of 'balanced budgets' for governments. These are policies which owe their origins to the Chicago School and to Friedrich Hayek and Milton Friedman. They would have devastating impacts on the working population and those dependent on government welfare. So this book challenges the flawed, if well-meaning, approaches of civil society organisations that are steering many on the Left into, to my mind, an intellectual dead-end.

Challenging the economics profession

Part of the reason there is so much public confusion about money, banking and debt is that the economics profession stands aloof from the financial system, declines (on the whole) to understand or teach these subjects, and arrogantly blames others (including politicians and consumers) for financial crises. As evidence of this arrogance, Professor Steve Keen in *Debunking Economics* cites the words of Ben Bernanke, governor of the US Federal Reserve at the time of the crisis: 'the recent financial crisis was more a failure of economic engineering and economic management than of what I have called economic science.'[7]

The 'economic scientists' of the profession (and many on the Left) have also systematically ignored or downplayed the monetary theory and policies of the genius that was John Maynard Keynes – theory and policies that could have averted the 2007–09 crisis. Instead 'Keynesian' policies are derided as 'taxing and spending', even while Keynes's primary concern was with monetary policy (the management of the currency, the money supply and interest rates). He was concerned with prevention of crises, not cure. His great work was, after all titled *The General Theory of Employment, Interest and Money*. However, that did not mean that he did not attach importance to the deployment of fiscal policy (spending and taxation) as part of the 'cure' of a crisis. He simply wanted monetary policy to be well managed so as to ensure employment and prosperity and prevent crises. Because of the value of his monetary theory this book draws heavily on John Maynard Keynes's policies – still regarded as taboo by the economics establishment.

Keynes was a British intellectual whose only equal to my mind is Charles Darwin. Both revolutionised and brought greater understanding to the fields they investigated and worked in, to the discomfort of many of their contemporaries and peers. They have both met with extraordinary resistance, as the persistence of creationism in US schools shows;[8] and as demonstrated by the restoration of the classical school of economics in all university departments and even at Keynes's own alma mater, Cambridge University.

The failure to build on Keynes's radical understanding of the monetary system has to my mind led orthodox economists (and much of the political class) into the kind of irrational denial that characterises anti-Darwinian 'creationism'. Neglect of Keynes, I will argue, has come at a high cost: the unemployment and impoverishment of millions of people, recurring financial and economic crises, polarising inequality, social and political insurrections, and war. But this neglect should come as no surprise, as Keynes was ruthless in his approach to the subordination of the finance sector to the interests of wider society and actively campaigned for the 'euthanasia of the rentier'. He regarded the love of money for its own sake as 'a somewhat disgusting morbidity, one of those semi-criminal, semi-pathological propensities which one hands over with a kind of shudder to the specialist in mental diseases'.[9]

He made many enemies among the finance sector and its friends in economics departments, so it is no wonder that they have buried his ideas and allowed the neoliberal equivalent of 'creationism' to prevail in our universities and economics departments.

So while much has changed since he died, nevertheless his understanding of the fundamentals of the monetary system remain relevant and can still inform sound policy-making. Furthermore adoption of Keynes's monetary theory and associated policies will, in my view, be vital to the restoration of economic and environmental stability and to the restoration of social justice.

So, besides a wider understanding of the finance system, what is to be done to restore economic prosperity, financial stability and social justice?

The answer in my view can be summed up in one line: bring offshore capitalism back onshore.

For a regulatory democracy to manage a financial system in the interests of the population as a whole, and not just the mobile, globalised few, requires that offshore capital be brought back onshore by means of capital control. Only then will it be possible for central banks to manage interest rates and keep them low across the spectrum of lending – essential to the health and prosperity of any economy. It is also, as I explain later in the book, essential to the management of toxic emissions and the ecosystem. Only then will it be possible to manage credit creation, and limit the rise of unsustainable consumption and debts. And only then will it be possible to enforce democratically determined taxation rules, and manage tax evasion. Democratic policy-making – on taxation, pensions, criminal justice, interest rates, etc. – requires boundaries and borders. A borderless country could not enforce taxation rates, or agree which citizens should be eligible for pensions, or detain criminals. But freewheeling, global financiers abhor boundaries and regulatory democracies.

There are brave economists who have for many years argued that states should have the power to manage flows of capital. They include professors Dani Rodrik and Kevin P. Gallagher, and have lately been joined by some orthodox economists, including the highly respected Professor Hélène Rey, who has argued that the armoury of macroprudential tools should not exclude capital control. Until now their voices have been eclipsed by effective lobbying from financiers on Wall Street and the City of London. At the same time the arguments for capital control have not attracted support from the Left or from social democratic parties. On the contrary, most social democratic governments both accept and reinforce a form of hyperglobalisation.

To bring global capital back onshore would be transformational of the global monetary order. Only then could we hope to restore stability, prosperity and social justice to a polarised and dangerously unequal world. Only then could we hope to manage the challenge of climate change.

CHAPTER I

Credit Power

Modern finance is generally incomprehensible to ordinary men and women ... The level of comprehension of many bankers and regulators is not significantly higher. It was probably designed that way. Like the wolf in the fairy tale: 'All the better to fleece you with.'

Satyajit Das, *Traders, Guns and Money* (2010)

Finance must be the servant, and the intelligent servant, of the community and productive industry; not their stupid master.

National Executive Committee of the
British Labour Party (June 1944),
Full Employment and Financial Policy

The global finance sector today exercises extraordinary power over society and in particular over governments, industry and labour. Players in financial markets dominate economic policy-making, undermine democratic decision-making, and have helped financialise almost all sectors of the economy (except perhaps faith organisations). Financiers have made vast capital gains by siphoning rent (interest) from debt, but also by effortlessly draining rent from pre-existing assets such as land, property, natural resource monopolies (water, electricity), forests, works of art, race horses, brands and companies. As Michael Hudson writes, 'the financial sector's aim is not to minimize the cost of roads, electric power, transportation, water or education, but to maximize what can be charged as monopoly rent.'[1]

Bankers and hedge funders in Wall Street and other financial centres have made determined efforts to weaken democratic institutions by weakening financial regulation, lobbying for cuts in capital gains taxes and for reversals in progressive taxation. And the sector has used capital mobility to transfer capital gains offshore, to havens like Panama, London, Delaware (US), Luxembourg, Switzerland and British Overseas Territories. Indeed the global finance sector has every reason to be triumphant. It has succeeded in capturing, effectively looting and then subordinating governments and their taxpayers to the interests of footloose and unaccountable financiers and financial markets.

Geoffrey Ingham, the Cambridge sociologist, describes the power the sector now wields as 'despotic'.[2]

Unfortunately, because of its opacity and because of deliberate efforts to obscure its activities, there is widespread ignorance of how money is created, of credit's and debt's role in the economy, of banking and of how the financial and monetary system works. Most orthodox economists are at fault, because many ignore money, debt and the banking system altogether in their university courses and in their analyses of economic activity. In the words of one leading international economist who will remain anonymous, money or credit is 'a matter of third-order importance'. Most economists (both 'classical', 'neoclassical' and many that are supposedly 'Keynesians') treat money as if it were 'neutral' or simply a 'veil' over economic transactions. They regard bankers as simply intermediaries between savers and borrowers, and the rate of interest as a 'natural' rate responding to the demand for, and supply of money. As a result of this blind spot for money and banking, it should come as no surprise that most mainstream economists failed to correctly analyse or predict the Great Financial Crisis of 2007–09. Just as worrying, this disregard for fundamental questions relating to the financing of the economy has meant that debates about finance's 'despotic power', and in whose interests the monetary system is managed, have long been neglected. Some think this neglect is not accidental. It has, after all, enabled global finance capital to thrive, untroubled by close academic or public scrutiny.

But it has also led to grave misunderstandings. One of the most serious is the often repeated accusation that central banks 'print money' and thereby cause inflation. While it is true that central banks are responsible for both the issue and the maintenance of the value of the currency, they are not responsible for 'printing' the nation's money supply. As the then-governor of the Bank of England Mervyn King once explained, it is the *private* commercial banking system that 'prints' 95 percent of broad money (money in any form including bank or other deposits as well as notes and coins) while the central bank issues only about 5 percent or less.[3] In a lightly regulated system, it is private commercial banks that hold the power to dispense or withhold finance from those active in the economy.[4] Yet neoliberal economists largely ignore private money 'printing' and aim their fire instead at governments and state-backed central bankers whom they regularly accuse of stoking inflation. The monetarist blind spot for the link between private banks' money creation and inflation goes some way to explaining why Mrs Thatcher's economic advisers found they could not control inflation.[5] They had aimed only to target the *public* money supply – government spending and borrowing. Monetarist economists presided over the deregulation of lending standards in *private* commercial bank credit creation. This deregulation freed up bankers to embark on a lending spree which in turn fuelled inflation. It is the reason why Mrs Thatcher presided over an inflation rate of 21.9 percent in her first year of office. Only in the fourth year of her administration did inflation come down below the inherited rate, and then only as a result of severe 'austerity'. As William Keegan explains, the 'defunct (monetarist) economic doctrine led not only to a rise in inflation, but also to a savage squeeze on the British economy and to escalating unemployment.'[6]

The blind spot for the *private* creation of credit is part of an ideology that holds that public is bad and private is good. 'Free, competitive markets' that are both invisible and unaccountable, it is argued, can be trusted to manage the global finance sector and the world's economies. This thinking stems not just from an almost religious belief in 'free' markets, but also from a contempt for the democratic regulatory state – a contempt actively expressed by supporters of the Thatcher and Reagan governments of the 1980s, and by elected politicians ever since.

Management of the monetary system

While the creation of money 'out of thin air' is a fascinating and, to many, a fresh discovery, what matters is not finance *per se*, but rather, I will argue, the management or *control* over what Keynes called the 'elastic production of money'. There should be no objection to a monetary system in which commercial banks create finance needed for productive, employment-generating activity in the real economy. Indeed, commercial banks have a critical role to play in risk assessing, providing and then smoothing the flow of finance around the economy. Bank clerks have critical roles to play in managing myriad social relationships between debtors and the bank, and in assessing the risk of the bank's potential borrowers. While I am not opposed to the nationalisation of banks, civil servants in big bureaucracies are not best suited to undertake risk assessments of the many applications for loans made at banks each working day. I can think of better functions for our civil servants than assessing Mrs Jones's application for a mortgage, Mr Smith's application for a car loan, and a corner shop's application for an overdraft.

However, the power of private, commercial bankers to create and distribute finance at a 'price' (the rate of interest) they themselves determine is a great power. It is bestowed and backed by public infrastructure (the central bank, the legal system and the system of public taxation). It is a power that must therefore be carefully and rigorously regulated by publicly accountable institutions if it is not to become 'despotic'. The authorities should ensure that finance or credit is deployed fairly, at sustainable rates of interest, for sound, affordable economic activity, and not for risky and often systemically dangerous speculation. Above all, the great power bestowed on banks by society – the power to create money 'out of thin air' – should not be used for their own self-enrichment. Nor should banks use retail customer deposits or loans as collateral for the bank's own borrowing and speculation. That much is common sense, and should inform a democratic society's regulatory oversight of the banks.

The value of a sound banking system

While it is controversial in some circles to assert this, it is my view that monetary and financial systems are among human society's greatest cultural and economic achievements. The creation of money by a well-developed monetary and banking system, first in Florence, then in Holland, and finally in Britain with the founding of the Bank of England in 1694, can be viewed as a great civilizational advance. As a result of the development of these sound monetary systems, there was no longer a shortage of finance for private enterprise or for the public good. Bold adventurers did not need to rely on rich and powerful 'robber barons' for finance. Instead bankers disbursed loans on the basis of a borrower's credibility. This led to the greater availability of finance for a wider range of private and public entrepreneurs, and not just for select groups of the powerful. The new and slowly developed monetary and financial systems both democratised access to finance, and simultaneously lowered the 'price' or rate of interest charged on loans. As a result, there was no shortage of money to invest in and create economic activity and employment. And that is why today, for those who live in societies with sound, developed monetary systems, there need never be insufficient money to tackle, for example, energy insecurity and climate change. There need never be a shortage of money to solve the great scourges of humanity: poverty, disease and inequality; to ensure humanity's prosperity and wellbeing; to finance the arts and wider culture; and to ensure the 'liveability' of the ecosystem.

The real shortages we face are first, humanity's capacity: the limits of our individual, social and collective integrity, imagination, intelligence, organisation and muscle. Second, the physical limits of the ecosystem. These are real limitations. However, the social relationships which create money, and sustain trust, need not be in short supply in a well-regulated and managed monetary system.

Within a sound financial system we can afford what we can do. Money enables us to do what we can within our limited natural and human resources. This is because money or credit does not exist as a *result* of economic activity, as many believe. Like the spending on our credit card, money *creates* economic activity.

Savings as a consequence, not precondition of credit

When young people leave school, obtain a job, and at the end of the month earn income, they wrongly assume that their newfound income is the result of work, or economic activity. This leads to the widespread assumption that money exists as *a consequence* of economic activity. In fact, with very rare exceptions, it is credit that, when issued by the bank and deposited as new money in a firm's account, kick-starts activity. It was probably a bank overdraft that helped pay the wage she earned in that first job. Hopefully, her employment created additional economic activity (because, for example, she helped produce and sell widgets) which in turn generated *income* and savings needed to reduce the overdraft, repay the debt and afford her wage.

In a well-managed financial system, money provides the catalyst, the finance needed for innovation, for production and for job creation. In a well-managed economy, money is invested in productive, not speculative, economic activity. In a stable system, economic activity (investment, employment) generates profits, wages and income that can be used for repayment of the original credit.

Of course, there must be constraints on the 'elastic production' of this social construct that we call money. This is because bankers and their clients can help trigger inflation on the one hand, and deflation on the other. When bankers create more credit/debt than can usefully be employed by an economy, this can result in 'too much money chasing too few goods or services' – i.e. inflation. Equally, the private banking system is capable of contracting the amount of credit created. This shrinks the supply of broad money, thereby *deflating* activity and employment. If the banking system is properly regulated by public authorities, and operated in the interests of the economy as a whole, there need never be a shortage of finance for sound productive activity.

That is why sound banking and modern monetary systems – just as sanitation, clean air and water – can be a great 'public good'. They can be used to ensure stability and prosperity, to advance development and to finance ecological sustainability, as I explain below. Managed badly, a banking system can fatally undermine social, political, economic and ecological goals, as they do in many low-income countries. Bankers and other lenders (including micro-lenders) can charge usurious, and ultimately unpayable, rates of interest on credit. By using their despotic power to withhold credit or finance from the economy, bankers and financiers can cause economic activity to contract, leading to the deflation of wages and prices, unemployment and social misery. Left to run amok, a banking and financial system can, and regularly does have a catastrophic impact on society and the ecosystem. Managed badly, a financial system can usurp and cannibalise society's democratic institutions.

We are living through a disastrous era in which the finance sector has expanded vastly – an era in which most financiers have virtually no direct relationship to the real economy's production of goods and services. Deregulation has enabled the sector to feed upon itself, to enrich its members and to detach its activities from the real economy. Productive actors in the real economy, the makers and creators, have periodically been flooded with 'easy if dear money' and have been just as frequently starved of *affordable* finance. This instability has led to increasingly frequent crises since the 'liberalisation' policies of the 1970s; and to prolonged failure since the financial crisis of 2007–09.

Many low-income countries are dogged by badly managed and lightly regulated financial systems, and therefore by a shortage of finance for commerce and production and for vital public services. This is in part because they lack the necessary public institutions (for example a sound central bank, a trusted criminal justice system, and a regulated accounting profession) and policies (including taxation policies) that underpin a properly functioning financial sector. No monetary and banking system can function well without a central bank, a system of regulation and of taxation; without sound accounting, and without a system of justice that enforces contracts and prevents fraud. But while low-income countries have been encouraged to open up their capital and trade markets and to invite in *private* wealth, they have been discouraged or blocked outright in their efforts to build sound *public* institutions and policies to manage their monetary and taxation systems. Above all, they have been discouraged from regulating the creation of credit ('leave it to the market') at affordable rates of interest by the private banking sector, or from managing financial flows in and out of their economy.

The role of robber barons

In countries with weak regulatory institutions and systems, entrepreneurs are obliged to turn for loan finance to those who have acquired – by fair means or foul – stocks of wealth or capital. Poor country governments turn to institutions like the IMF and World Bank or to the international capital markets for foreign hard currency. As a consequence of dependence on both domestic and international 'robber barons', money is expensive ('dear'). It is lent by powerful foreign creditors with the authority to create credit in a stable currency. Alternatively it is lent by those individuals or companies with savings or a surplus, invariably at high real rates of interest – rates that often exceed the income or returns that can be made on the investment. If it is borrowed in foreign currency, then volatility in currency movements can both increase the cost of the loan but also diminish those costs. But volatility is a deterrent to promising enterprises. As a result of the need to borrow in foreign currency, a poor country's innovative sectors can be held back, unemployment and under-employment will remain high, and poverty can become entrenched.

Yet it does not have to be this way. Monetary systems and financial markets have been cut loose from the ties that bind them to the real economy, and to society's relationships, its values and needs. That is largely because monetary systems have been captured by wealthy elites who, with the collusion of regulators and elected politicians, have undermined society's democratic institutions and now govern the financial system in their own narrow and perverse interests.

Opposition to regulatory democracy

Of the orthodox economists who show an interest in the finance sector, most are opposed to managing and regulating finance in the interests of society as a whole. Acting consciously or unconsciously on behalf of creditor interests, they effectively provide justification for 'easy' (that is unregulated) but 'dear' (at high, real rates of interest) credit. This, I will argue, is the worst possible combination for society and the ecosystem as high and rising real rates of interest require high and rising rates of return from investment, from labour and from the earth's finite assets.

Most orthodox economists also have an unhealthy dislike of the state, which they accuse of 'rent-seeking' while simultaneously ignoring the rent-seeking of the private sector. As recently as October 2008 former governor of the US Federal Reserve Alan Greenspan made the orthodoxy explicit under cross-examination by a Congressional committee, chaired by Henry Waxman.[7] The chairman reminded Mr Greenspan that he had once said, 'I do have an ideology. My judgement is that free, competitive markets are by far the unrivalled way to organise economies. We've tried regulation. None meaningfully worked.' Greenspan later went on to explain, '[I had] found a flaw in the model that I perceived as the critical functioning structure that defines how the world works, so to speak ... That's precisely the reason I was shocked, because I had been going for forty years or more with very considerable evidence that it was working exceptionally well.'

Over this period, and thanks to the pervasive influence of the economic orthodoxy espoused by Mr Greenspan and others, western governments used markets as 'the unrivalled way to organise economies'. 'Light-touch regulation', 'outsourcing', 'globalisation' and other policy changes were cheered on as ways to effectively transfer control of the public good that is the monetary system to private wealth. The orthodoxy conceded two great powers to private bankers and financiers: first, the ability to create, price and manage credit without effective supervision or regulation; second, the ability to 'manage' global financial flows across borders – and to do so out of sight of the regulatory authorities. By way of this shift, democratic and accountable public authorities handed effective control over the economy – over employment, welfare and incomes – to remote and unaccountable financial markets.

This hand-over of great financial authority took place by stealth. There was virtually no public or academic debate about the transfer of power away from public, accountable regulators to private interests. Instead the public were offered reassuring platitudes about the ability of markets to 'discipline' the sector, if self-regulation failed. Competition, we were told, would eliminate cheating and fraud.

The outcome was entirely predictable. Individuals and corporations in the private finance sector made historically unprecedented capital and criminal gains. Vast wealth was extracted from those outside the sector. Those engaged in productive activity experienced falling output and unemployment. After liberalisation took hold in the 1970s, and as profits fell relative to earlier periods, unemployment rose across the world and wages declined as a share of GDP. Inequality exploded. Globally private debt expanded and exceeded global income. And financial crises proliferated as Professor Ken Rogoff and Carmen Reinhart have shown.

Trust and confidence in the banking system and in democratic and other public institutions waned. The reason is not hard to understand. The transfer of economic power away from public authority to private wealthy elites had placed key financiers beyond the reach of the law, of regulators or politicians. This loss of democratic power hollowed out democratic institutions – parliaments and congresses – while 'privatisation' diminished whole sectors of the economy that had been subject to democratic oversight.

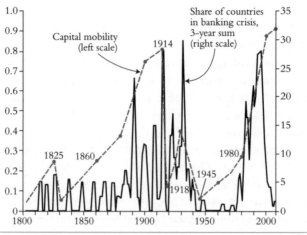

Source: This Time is Different: A Panoramic View of Eight Centuries of Financial Crises by Carmen M. Reinhart, University of Maryland and NBER; and Kenneth S. Rogoff, Harvard University and NBER.

Fig. 1. Financial crises during periods of high capital mobility after financial liberalisation.

The economics profession and the universities stood aloof, as enormous power was concentrated in the hands of small groups of reckless financiers. Academic economists tended to focus myopically on *micro*economic issues and lose sight of the *macro*economy. To this day, the academic economics profession remains distanced from the crisis, and almost irrelevant to its resolution.

Politicians and the media were dazed and confused by the finance sector's activities. Gillian Tett, one of the few journalists bold enough to explore and challenge the world of international financiers and creditors, blames a 'pattern of "social silence" … which ensured that the operations of complex credit were deemed too dull, irrelevant or technical to attract interest from outsiders, such as journalists and politicians.'[8] Finance was indeed too dull and arcane to attract the interest of mainstream feminism and environmentalism.

As a result of this 'social silence' citizens were unprepared for the crisis, and they remain on the whole ignorant of the workings of the financial system and its operations.

The experience of financial deregulation has shown that capitalism insulated from popular democracy degenerates into rent-seeking, criminality and grand corruption. As Karl Polanyi predicted in his famous book *The Great Transformation*, societies are building resistance to the 'self-regulating market comprising labour, land and money' – or market fundamentalism, even when blind resistance appears irrational.[9] In the US, as I write, the voters of the United States have sought protection from a demagogic president-elect who promised to defend them by erecting a wall between the United States and Mexico. In Europe, leaders that would impose authoritarian nationalist control over economies are gaining in popularity.

Just as in the 1920s and '30s, societies are moving towards authoritarian leaders in the vain belief that their new 'masters' will provide protection from 'the stupid master' identified by the British Labour Party in 1944: deregulated, globalised finance.

CHAPTER 2

The Creation of Money

*Credit is the purchasing power so often mentioned in eco-
nomic works as being one of the principal attributes of money,
and, as I shall try to show, credit and credit alone is money.
Credit and not gold or silver is the one property which all
men seek, the acquisition of which is the aim and object of
all commerce. There is no question but that credit is far older
than cash.*

Mitchell Innes, 'What Is Money?'
The Banking Law Journal, May 1913

*The notion – developed by Adam Smith – that the wealth of a
nation is measured not by monetary values, but by its capacity
to produce goods and services.*

Andrea Terzi, INET Conference, April 2015

Bernanke breaks a taboo

The date was 15 March 2009. Just months before, the
bankruptcy of an investment bank, Lehman's, had led to
financial mayhem. The 2007–09 Global Financial Crisis was
in its earliest stages. But on that day something historically
unprecedented happened. Ben Bernanke gave the first-ever
broadcast interview by a Federal Reserve bank governor to
an American journalist. The journalist was Scott Pelly. The
show was CBS's iconic *60 Minutes*.

The day before the interview, Mr Bernanke's Fed – the
world's most powerful central bank – had undertaken
something exceptional as part of a routine monetary operation. The board had agreed to loan $85 billion to AIG – an

insurance company that wasn't a bank at all, and should never have had an account with the Fed. Under both Governors Greenspan's and Bernanke's watch, AIG had accumulated (in some cases fraudulently) extraordinary liabilities as a player in the $62 trillion credit-default swaps (CDS) market. Mr Bernanke explained to Scott Pelly that the Fed's $85 billion bailout of AIG, which was one of several loans to AIG, was a short-term, urgent measure to prevent the systemic failure of the *global* finance sector.

But Pelley was puzzled by it all and posed this question. Where had the Fed found the money? Had the $85 billion been tax money? 'No', said Bernanke firmly. 'It's not tax money. The banks have accounts with the Fed, much the same way that you have an account in a commercial bank. So, to lend to a bank, we simply use the computer to mark up the size of the account that they have with the Fed.' The sum of $85 billion dollars, expressed in numerals with nine noughts – $85,000,000,000 – was transferred to AIG's account in just an instant after all eleven numbers had simply been tapped into a Fed computer.

While the AIG sum was a remarkable amount of money, the action itself – of entering numbers into a computer and transferring the sums to a borrower's bank account – is unremarkable. It is, as Bernanke made clear, what commercial bankers do every day, each time they deposit a personal or business loan in a bank account. Furthermore, it is what private commercial bankers have been doing (albeit at first with fountain pen entries into ledgers, rather than by tapping numbers on a computer keyboard) since before the founding of the Bank of England in 1694.

It is a great power. A power that bankers can only exercise thanks to the backing of a society's taxpayers and of publicly financed institutions. As such it is a power that should be wielded in the interests of society as a whole, and not just in the vested interests of the privately wealthy.

Money: the means *by* which we exchange goods and services

While the orthodox or neoclassical school of economists pay little attention to 'neutral' money in designing models of the economy, they also conceive of it as akin to a commodity. Money, in their view, is representative of a tangible asset or scarce commodity, like gold or silver. As with any commodity, for example corn, money in the orthodox view can be set aside or saved, accumulated and then loaned out. Savers lend their surplus to borrowers, and bankers are mere intermediaries between savers and borrowers.

While it is true that some institutions (savings banks, credit unions, British building societies of old, today's crowd-funders) collect savings and lend these out, commercial bankers have not acted as intermediaries between borrowers and savers, between 'patient' borrowers and 'impatient' lenders, since before the founding of the Bank of England in 1694.

Furthermore, because neoclassical economists conceive of money as having (like gold or silver) a scarcity value, they theorise as if money is subject to market forces, as if money's 'price' – the rate of interest – is a consequence of the supply of and demand for money. Many argue that like commodities, money or savings can become scarce.

But money is not like a commodity, and to define it as such is to create a 'false commodity' as Karl Polanyi argued.[1] On the contrary, with the development of sound monetary systems in developed economies, there is never a shortage of money for society's most important needs. Instead the relevant question is: who controls the creation of money? And to what end is money created?

The gap between the orthodox or neoclassical understanding of the nature of money and interest, and for example, the modern Keynesian or Minskyian (American economist Hyman Minsky [1919–96]) understanding of money and interest, is as wide and profound as that between sixteenth-century Ptolemaic and Copernican concepts of the heavens. Closing the gap in knowledge is almost impossible because 'classical' economists are, and have long been, dominant within universities. They are particularly influential in financial institutions, where their theories are both welcomed and encouraged. These institutions long ago marginalised the monetary theories of, for example, the great Scottish economist John Law (1671–1729) who explained the nature of money succinctly back in 1705. He was followed by Henry Thornton (1760–1815) and Henry Dunning MacLeod (1821–1902). John Maynard Keynes (1883–1946) built on these theories and developed practical policies for officials and politicians to implement. However, even then mainstream orthodox economists found his monetary theories and policies challenging, as Joseph Schumpeter explained in his *History of Economic Analysis* over sixty years ago:

> it proved extraordinarily difficult for economists to recognise that bank loans and bank investments do create deposits ... And even in 1930, when the large majority had been converted and accepted the doctrine as a matter of course, Keynes rightly felt it necessary to re-expound and to defend the doctrine at some length ... and some of the most important aspects cannot be said to be fully understood even now.[2]

A small group of distinguished economists all understood that money as part of a developed monetary system is not, and never has taken the form of a commodity. Instead money and the rate of interest are both *social constructs*: social relationships and social arrangements based primarily and ultimately on trust. The thing we call money has its original basis in belief. Credit is a word based on the Latin word *credo*: I believe. 'I believe you will pay, or repay me now or at some point in the future.' Money and its 'price' – the rate of interest – became the measure of that trust and/or promise. Or, if trust is absent, the measure of a lack of trust. If the banker does not fully trust a customer to repay, they will demand more as collateral or in interest payments.

Money in this view is not the thing *for* which we exchange goods and services but *by* which we undertake this exchange, as John Law famously argued in 1705.[3]

To understand this, think of your credit card. There is no money in most credit card accounts before a user begins to spend. All that exists is a social contract with a banker: a promise or obligation made to the banker to repay the debt incurred as a result of spending on your card, at a certain time in the future and at an agreed rate of interest. And when 'money' is spent on your credit card, you do not exchange the card for the products you purchase. This is because money is not like barter. No, the card stays in your purse. Instead, the credit card, and the trust on which it is based, gives you the power to purchase a product or service. It is the means by which you acquire *purchasing power*.

The spending on a card is expenditure created 'out of thin air'. The intangible 'credit' is nothing more than the bank's and the retailer's belief that the owner of the card and her bank will honour an agreement to repay. As such, all credit and money is a social relationship of trust between those undertaking a transaction: between a banker and its customers; between buyers and sellers; between debtors and creditors. Money is not, and never has been, a commodity like a card, or oil, or gold – although coins and notes have, like credit cards, been used as a convenient *measure* of the trust between individuals engaged in transactions. So if a banker trusts one customer more than most others, they will be given a gold or platinum card. If a banker does not have trust in the customer's ability to pay, they will not be granted a credit card or may be given one with a very low limit. As a result, that customer will lose purchasing power.

Faith, belief and trust – that someone can be assessed as reliable and honest, and their proposed spending or investment sound – is at the heart of all money transactions. Without trust, monetary systems collapse and transactions dry up.

The good news: savings are not needed for investment

The miracle of a developed monetary economy is this: *savings are not necessary to fund purchases or investment.* Those entrepreneurs or individuals in need of funds for investment need not rely on finance from individuals that set aside their income in a savings bank or under the mattress. Instead they can obtain finance from a private commercial bank. This availability of finance in a monetary economy is in contrast to a poor, under-developed, non-monetary economy where savings are the only source of finance for investment, and where inevitably, there is no money for society's most urgent needs.

The economist Andrea Terzi explains the difference between a monetary and non-monetary economy well:

> When people save in the form of a real commodity, like corn, the decision to save is a fully personal matter: if you have acquired a given amount of corn, you have the privilege of consuming it, storing it, wasting it, as you please, without this directly affecting other people's consumption of corn. *Only if you decide to lend it will you establish a relationship with others.*
>
> In a monetary economy, saving is not a real quantity that anyone can independently own, like corn or gold or a collection of rare stamps. In a monetary economy, as opposed to a non-monetary economy, saving is an act that [establishes a relationship with others] … in the form of a financial *claim.*
>
> Unlike a commodity such as corn, financial saving always appears as a financial relationship, as it exists only as a claim

on others, in the form of banknotes, bank deposits or other financial assets. Personal savings are claims of one economic unit on another, and any change in savings entails a change in the relationship between the 'saver' and other economic units. This does not appear on national accounts, which only expose aggregate values.

If we then look at savings by zooming out of the individual unit and considering the interconnections between units and between sectors, we find that each penny saved must correspond to a debt of equal size. A banknote is a central bank's liability. A bank deposit is a bank's liability. A government security is a government liability. A corporate bond is a private company liability, and so on. This means that when we discuss financial savings we are also discussing debt. Every penny saved is someone else's liability ... every penny saved is somebody's debt.

In a monetary economy, savings do not fund; they need to be funded.[4]

To sum up: in a monetary economy saving is different from the business of building up a surplus of corn, and then lending it on. The corn can be saved without it ever affecting others. However, saving in an economy based on money always 'affects others' because it is *always* an act that sets up a financial relationship with others: a claim. Claims can take the form of an asset or a liability. So for example, when a central bank issues a dollar bill to a private bank, it has a duty (liability) to deliver the value of that currency to the bank that applies for it. The bank then has an asset (the dollar bill), but also owes something (a liability) to the central bank. When a commercial bank makes a deposit in a client's account, it has a duty to disburse money to the person that applied for a loan (sometimes in the form of cash). The borrower has an asset, the money deposited, but also a liability, a duty to pay back the loan, and so on. These are the relationships – of credit and debt, between owners of liabilities and assets – that are fundamental to a monetary economy, and that generate the income and savings needed for investment, employment and all manner of useful and important activities.

Of course these monetary relationships must be carefully managed to ensure that they do not become unbalanced, unfair or unstable. Money lent must not be burdened by high, unpayable real rates of interest. Above all, credit creation must be managed to ensure that loans do not evolve into mountains of unpayable debt. The point of managing these relationships is to maintain equilibrium between those engaging in financial transactions. In other words, to maintain fairness between debtors and creditors, to ensure not just prosperity, but economic stability. If well managed, these claims, the social relationships within a monetary system, can provide all the finance that society needs. *If well managed, there need never be a shortage of money for society's most urgent projects.* If well managed, debt is not compounded by usurious rates of interest, and does not accumulate well beyond the borrower's, the economy's or the ecosystem's capacity to repay.

It is the case that if savings in an economy are to expand, then it will be necessary for debt to expand too. It is when the debt exceeds the capacity to repay, that it becomes a burden on individuals, firms and the economy as a whole. To avoid the exploitative nature of debt, two conditions must be imposed on commercial bankers. First, the rate of interest on loans should always be low enough to ensure repayment (for more on this see Chapter 3). Second, loans should be made for activities that are judged to be productive, and likely to generate employment and income. Ideally, lending for speculative activity should be discouraged or banned. Questions that bankers should ask of loan applicants should include: will the finance created by the debt be used to create employment and other activities that will generate income? Will the financial claims be used for productive and sustainable activity? If the creation of debt does meet these criteria, it is unlikely to become a burden on the borrower, and will be repayable, over time.

As noted above, less borrowing implies less money in circulation and therefore fewer savings. Such a shrinkage of available finance in due course takes the form of falling prices, falling wages and incomes – in other words, the contraction of credit implies deflationary pressures. Falling prices apply pressure on profits and lead to bankruptcies, which likely lead to job losses. The unemployed are even less likely to borrow and spend, which means that the nation's income contracts even further.

What is needed in the economically depressed circumstances outlined above, is for governments to begin to create money or savings by issuing debt that will finance investment in projects involving the new production of goods or services that in turn create employment. These activities will then provide both private incomes and the tax revenue with which the public debt can be repaid.

Savings, as Andrea Terzi writes, need to be funded, and at times of private sector weakness, the best the way to fund savings would be for governments or private banks to issue new debt.

To sum up: credit (or debt) is how all money is created or produced in the first instance. With the development of sound and well-managed monetary systems, there need be no limit on the availability of finance or credit for sustainable, income-generating activity. As Keynes argued, what we create, we can afford.[5] The credit system enables us to do what we can do within the physical limits imposed by our own, the economy's and the ecosystem's resources.

That is the good news: a well-developed monetary system can finance very big projects, projects whose financing would far exceed an economy's total savings, squirrelled away in

THE PRODUCTION OF MONEY

piggy banks or other institutions. That means a society based on a sound monetary system could 'afford' a free education and health system; could fund support for the arts as well as defence; could tackle diseases or bail out banks in a financial crisis. While we may be short of the physical and human resources needed to transform economies away from fossil fuels, society need never be short of the financial relationships – the claims we make on each other – needed for the urgent and vast changes required to ensure the environment remains liveable. However, if a monetary system is not managed and operates instead in the interests of just a few, it can have a catastrophic economic, political and environmental impact.

2014: The Bank of England reaffirms the theory of money

To affirm the theories of economists like Law, Thornton, MacLeod, Keynes, Schumacher, Galbraith and Minsky, and to confirm Bernanke's point, the Bank of England published two articles on the nature of money in their January 2014 *Quarterly Bulletin.*[6] The articles were met with delight by monetary reformers and indifference by many mainstream economists.

The Bank's economists made clear that most of the money in the modern economy is 'printed' by private commercial banks making loans – and is not created by central banks. In other words, almost all money in circulation originates as credit or debt in the *private* banking system. Rather than banks acting as intermediaries and lending out deposits that were placed with them, it is the act of lending itself that creates deposits or bank money, and is also a debt, the Bank's staff explained. Of course this bank money is not actually printed by the private bank; only the central bank has the legal authority to print money and mint coins. The money created by a loan – bank money – is simply digitally transferred from one private bank account to another. The only

24

evidence of its existence is in the numbers printed on a bank statement. Of the total amount of money created, only a tiny proportion is normally converted into tangible money in the form of notes and coins, or cash.

For private commercial bankers operating within a monetary economy, the relevant consideration is not the availability of existing savings, but the viability of the borrower, her project, her collateral and the assessment of whether the project will generate income with which she can repay the credit/debt.

And yes, the Bank of England confirmed that in a monetary economy the money multiplier (the percentage of deposits that banks are required to hold as reserves against lending) is an incorrect account of the lending process. Bank lending is not constrained by 'reserves'. The assumption that banks hold reserves equal to a fraction of their lending – 'fractional reserve banking' – is wrong. Bank 'reserves' are not savings in the sense we understand them. They are resources (resembling an overdraft) made available only to the bankers licensed by the central bank. They are used to facilitate the 'clearing' process for settling deposits and liabilities between banks at the end of each day. Central bank reserves never leave the banking system to enter the real economy. While central bank reserves may help to free up the balance sheets of banks and other associated financial institutions, they cannot be used to lend on to firms or individuals in the non-bank economy.

Instead as Mr Bernanke explained, private bankers – in both the formal banking system and the 'shadow banking' sector, the newly developed finance sector where credit creation is not subject to regulatory oversight – create the credit which is used as money. They do so 'out of thin air' by entering numbers into a computer, and by obtaining a promise to repay at a certain time and at a certain rate of interest. They first obtain collateral (e.g. property or other assets) as a guarantee against the liability they incur when they create money. Second, they agree a rate of interest and a repayment term with the borrower, which is then given legal force by way of a contract. Finally, the banker enters numbers into a computer or a ledger and deposits the loan in a borrower's bank account.

This new money or credit is known as 'bank money'. Its quality, acceptability and validity is simply due to its ability to facilitate transactions. It is almost effortless activity, and invites Keynes's famous question, 'Why then ... if banks can create credit, should they refuse any reasonable request for it? And why should they charge a fee for what costs them little or nothing?'[7]

What about notes and coins?

While banks in deregulated systems are not on the whole constrained in their ability to create credit, there is one thing bankers cannot do: they are not licensed to issue notes and coins as legal tender. Only the publicly backed central bank can issue the legal, tangible currency of a nation as notes and coins. So if Joanna Public takes out a mortgage for, say, £300,000 and needs £3,000 in cash, the commercial bank has to apply to the central bank for the notes and coins she wishes to withdraw. The remaining £297,000 of credit is granted as intangible bank money, and is deposited digitally, via bank transfer, in Joanna's account.

It is important to understand that central banks currently place no limit on the cash made available to private commercial banks to satisfy a loan application. (There is, however, a move to 'ban' cash but that is for a later discussion). Indeed the central bank provides cash *on demand* to private commercial bankers, and places no limits on the cash, bank money, or credit that can be created by commercial banks.

Although the demand for cash is now falling, during the long boom the demand for credit accelerated – and central bankers turned a blind eye. They placed no limits on the quantity of credit created, nor did they offer guidance to private bankers on the quality of credit issued, that is, on what private credit must be used *for.* So bankers were free not only to lend for productive, income-generating activity, but also for risky, speculative activity, that need not necessarily generate a steady stream of income.

Private borrowers control the money supply

Of course there is more to the business of lending than just depositing a loan in a bank account. Borrowers (and lenders) have to be kept honest. Borrowers have to offer up sufficient collateral, and, to guarantee their trustworthiness, sign a legal and enforceable contract that upholds their promise to repay over a given period of time and at a rate of interest – the 'price' of a loan. The banker in turn has to honour the obligation to provide the loan or deposit at either an agreed fixed or variable rate of interest.

Borrowing, it goes without saying, is a two-way process. The borrower invariably triggers the loan, not the commercial banker (though the banker may offer inducements). The loan applicant can be an individual, corner shop, or global corporation. Once the application is made, the banker or creditor makes a risk assessment and consequently agrees or blocks the loan application. Only once a borrower offers collateral and an agreement to repay will a banker agree to extend credit. (Although lending via credit cards does not require the posting of collateral, prudent bankers should take care to assess a customer's future income flows before granting credit cards, and all bankers compensate for the lack of collateral by charging very high rates of interest on the card.)

It is, of course, the case that bankers, including central bankers, influence the money supply. They do this by raising the cost of lending and discouraging borrowers and thereby contracting the supply of money, or by easing lending conditions, encouraging borrowing and expanding the supply. And in all cases, it is individual commercial bankers that have the power to approve or decline loan applications. Private bankers, by agreeing to or denying loans, have enormous power over decisions that would increase or decrease investment, economic activity and employment.

Nevertheless, while bankers exercise great influence over the economy, they are dependent on borrowers within the real economy to exercise the (licensed) power to create credit or bank money. The nation's money supply can therefore be described as a bottom-up process. Bankers depend on borrowers with collateral to apply for a loan before they can disburse credit in the form of bank money or bank deposits. And the economy depends on borrowers for the expansion (or contraction) of the money supply. If borrowers lack confidence in their own ability to repay, or in the health of the economy, they will hold back, and at an aggregate level the money supply will contract. If borrowers are confident, they may take the risk of borrowing. If they're euphoric and believe the hype about rising prices, they may even borrow recklessly. Their borrowing, at an aggregate level, will expand the money supply.

In this way, governments and other institutions can depress the demand for loans, or they can help create a climate of confidence, optimism or euphoria to encourage borrowing and, with it, the supply of savings and money. However, the public authorities cannot actually *control* the money supply. That is up to the nation's borrowers.

Banks and bankruptcy
If bankers can create credit out of thin air, I hear readers ask, *how can they be bankrupted?* Easily, is the answer, especially if over time, they fail to pay attention to the liabilities on their balance sheets.

When a banker elicits a promise of loan repayment from a customer and then creates credit for the customer, this immediately becomes both a loan asset and a deposit liability on the bank's balance sheet. The loan is an asset because, over time, it will earn interest for the bank. The deposit is a liability because it is immediately owed by the bank to the customer or depositor who may withdraw it to make payments to another bank. (Time management is a critical function for bank managers.)

As explained above, the bank or lender has to manage assets and liabilities carefully to ensure funds are available when the depositor wishes to withdraw her deposit. The commercial bank does this in part by obtaining reserves from the central bank system each time it creates a deposit. These reserves are used for clearing and settling inter-bank financial transactions. The banking system as a whole has to manage financial transactions and ensure that cheques and other payments are cleared between those banks receiving payments and those making payments.

This is the critical role played by the central bank of any economy, for example the Bank of England, the US Federal Reserve, or the Bank of Japan. The central bank helps settle payments between banks by transferring central bank money (reserves) between the reserve accounts of those banks, debiting the accounts of banks making payments and crediting the accounts of banks receiving payments.

In normal times these payments cancel each other out, with only a small amount of central bank reserves needed for settlement at the end of the day. But bankers can get into difficulties, and times are not always normal. If owing to mismanagement a bank finds its liabilities begin to exceed its assets, then no amount of central bank reserves can help it: it is facing bankruptcy. If the public get wind of any difficulties, then there is a 'run' on the bank; deposits are quickly withdrawn, and liabilities begin to mount. Remember, most licensed banks have their customer deposits – up to a specified limit – guaranteed by the state, so deposits are on the whole, protected.

Until recently, commercial banks were prohibited from mixing their lending and deposit (commercial banking) arms with their more speculative investment arms. Then in 1999, President Clinton repealed the US Glass–Steagall Act (1933), on the advice of prominent economists like Professor Larry Summers and Treasury Secretary Robert Rubin. Other finance ministers and central bankers around the world soon followed President Clinton's example. Commercial bankers in global institutions were then freed up to link their own borrowing (often for speculative purposes) to the government-guaranteed retail deposits held in their banks. Because these two sides of banking became so closely integrated, borrowing for speculation by private bankers exposed all those who used the banking system to the risks taken by individual traders in the investment arms of the banks. This exposed the whole economy to major – or systemic – risks, costs and losses.

This reckless conduct helped precipitate the global financial crisis of 2007–09, when most of the big banks faced the threat of insolvency. They were bailed out by taxpayer-backed governments with barely a rap on the knuckles, and with very few 'terms and conditions'. To this day no banker has been jailed, or been held criminally responsible, or had to admit any wrongdoing for their role in precipitating global financial meltdown in 2007–09. Where fines have been administered, they have represented but a fraction of the cost to society of financial failure and wrongdoing. Andy Haldane, responsible for Financial Stability at the Bank of England, argued once that even if bankers were to compensate society for the losses endured, 'it is clear that banks would not have deep enough pockets to foot this bill.'[8]

Despite massive bailouts by taxpayer-backed central banks, it is my contention that, even as I write in 2016, global banks are still effectively insolvent. Government guarantees, cheap finance and quantitative easing, coupled with the manipulation of balance sheets, are all that appear to stand between today's 'too big to fail' banks and insolvency.

The deregulated financial system – and liquidity

Under our deregulated financial system, and despite the Great Financial Crisis of 2007–09, commercial bankers can create credit or liquidity (i.e. assets that can easily and readily be turned into cash) effectively without limit, and with few regulatory constraints. Central bankers and regulators no longer place limits on what money is created *for*. They are largely indifferent to the creation of credit for the purposes of speculation as opposed to purposive, productive, income-generating investment. And because speculation can be much more lucrative in the short-term (think Lottery winners) many investors prefer the capital gains made from speculation as opposed to the patient returns made on sound, productive investment.

The indifference and neglect of central bankers and the resulting system of deregulated finance has encouraged financiers in the ever-expanding 'shadow banking system' to create or 'securitise' more and more artificial or synthetic 'credit' products or assets. This has led (since the mid 1980s) to a new type of financial engineering de-linked from the real economy and known as the 'originate and distribute' model for packaging and 'originating' financial instruments or collateral. These assets are 'synthetic' in that, unlike property, works of art and other typical forms of collateral, they are created artificially from, for example, promises to repay. In the case of a phone company, this collateral could include bundles of customer contracts to pay phone bills for a period of time into the future. Or, in the case of a bank, the collateral could include contracts to pay back loans in the future. These 'promises' of future revenue streams can then be used to leverage substantial additional borrowing, generating substantial liquidity for those active in the shadow banking sector. Synthetic assets and the associated borrowing create tremendous wealth for speculators in these capital markets. They are often hidden from the public authorities and managed off balance sheets in 'special investment vehicles' or SIVs.

Problems occur when these unregulated 'promises' evaporate – and are defaulted upon. The so-called 'liquidity' quickly and dangerously dries up. A rush for the exits follows. Like a Ponzi scheme, those who get out first take most of the gains. The losers are left empty-handed.

Central bankers have, since the 1990s, turned a blind eye and largely failed to understand these and more innovative self-enriching activities. Shadow banking was only named and identified by the economist Paul McCulley as late as 2007, in a speech at the annual financial symposium hosted by the Kansas City Federal Reserve Bank in Jackson Hole, Wyoming.[9] Members of the shadow banking 'blind-eye brigade' include Alan Greenspan, who in 2004 said that under the deregulated system of credit creation, 'Not only have individual financial institutions become less vulnerable to shocks from underlying risk factors, but also the financial system as a whole has become more resilient.'[10]

Credit creation and Goethe's 'Sorcerer's Apprentice'

As argued above, to ensure that the monetary system addresses society's varied needs, credit (debt) creation must be managed to ensure it is offered at low real rates of interest, and used productively and sustainably to create employment, and with it savings, income and other revenues, part of which can be used to repay the debt. If the system is to remain stable and useful to society as a whole, then publicly accountable authorities must manage and regulate not just the creation of credit, but also the 'price' of that credit: the rate of interest. If, instead, the power of credit creation is left to the 'invisible hand' of the market, the consequences will be similar to those faced by Goethe's 'Sorcerer's Apprentice'.

Readers will recollect that, in the absence of the Sorcerer, the Apprentice misused his master's magic to conjure up water, brushes and pails that would magically undertake, without supervision, the work of cleaning up his master's studio. The result was chaos, with a proliferation of brushes and pails, and the flooding of the Sorcerer's workshop. So it is with unmanaged and unregulated credit creation; the result leads invariably to excessive credit creation, the inflation of assets, prices or wages, the build-up of unpayable debts, and then catastrophic failure of the financial system as debts are defaulted upon.

The 2006–07 sub-prime mortgage crisis in the US – when impoverished debtors defaulted on large sums of debt charged at high rates of interest – is a textbook example of how a system based on 'classical' monetary theory works. Economists reckoned that an excess supply of money ('the global savings glut') had, thanks to market forces, lowered the 'price' (interest rate) of money. Because of their conviction that bankers as dealers in money were like other intermediaries, simply acting as agents between buyers and sellers, economists thought banking activities could safely be guided by the 'invisible hand' of the market.

Private commercial bankers could hardly believe their luck. The Sorcerer – in the form of a financial regulator – had vacated a vast amount of monetary space and left them in charge of the magic of credit creation, not just in their own country, but globally; not just within the retail banking system, but outside the purview of regulators, in the 'shadow' banking system.

Bankers, creditors and financiers did what the Sorcerer's Apprentice had done: they went crazy. In the UK, households were encouraged to borrow 4 percent of GDP year after year. Irish households, according to Mark Carney, the governor of the Bank of England, borrowed more than twice that rate. Household debt peaked close to 100 percent of annual GDP in the UK and 120 percent in Ireland. And as the governor confirmed:

> This borrowing was largely for consumption and real estate investment rather than businesses and projects that would generate the earnings necessary to service those obligations. Property prices soared as a result.
>
> Such excesses were possible because a decade of non-inflationary, consistent expansion turned initially well-founded confidence into dangerous complacency. Beliefs grew that globalisation and technology would drive perpetual growth, and that the omniscience of central banks would deliver enduring stability. With a growing conviction that financial innovation had transformed risk into certainty, underwriting standards slipped from responsible to reckless and bank funding strategies from conservative to cavalier. Financial innovation made it easier to borrow. Bonus schemes valued the present and discounted the future.
>
> Banks operated in a heads-I-win-tails-you-lose bubble ...[11]

Inflation and deflation

The creation of credit and the supply of money faces two major constraints. First borrowers may become over-confident, even reckless, and borrow more than the economy's capacity can bear. Their unconstrained ('liberalised') financial euphoria would expand the money supply, much as a euphoric Sorcerer's Apprentice might fill a studio with pails, brushes and an overflow of water. 'Too much money chasing too few goods and services' would lead to inflation – which raises prices, but erodes the value of assets, including fixed incomes such as pensions and benefits. So public authorities have to manage credit creation by the private sector to prevent inflation, and the central bank can use its powers and leverage over the private banking system to discourage such lending. In 2014, for the first time in thirty years, the Bank of England restricted the amount that bankers could lend against property, and that home buyers could borrow, relative to their income.

Central bankers can also try and limit credit creation by offering 'guidance' to bankers on standards in lending, and by raising interest rates. Since liberalisation of credit creation in the late 1960s and early 1970s, the authorities have preferred the latter method as the sole way of managing credit creation.

Borrowers' euphoria poses a threat to the economy. However, risk-averse borrowers – fearful of the future and unwilling to borrow – pose a grave threat too. Too little borrowing leads to a contraction of the money supply, which in turn leads to disinflation (a reduction in the rate of inflation) or even deflation (a decrease in the general level of prices, when the inflation rate falls below 0 percent).

Both inflation and deflation pose real threats to the wider economy and to social and political stability. Deflation, if it becomes entrenched, is particularly difficult to reverse (witness Japan's deflated economy since 1990) as the public authorities have few tools with which to address deflationary pressures. That is why it is vital that credit creation is not left to the 'invisible hand' – to players in financial markets. In a democracy, it is the responsibility of 'the guardians of the nation's finances' – central bankers, finance ministers and treasury civil servants – to manage the almost effortless process of both credit creation and the rate of interest – for the benefit of the economy as a whole.

Private money's wealth dependent on public largesse
One of the great injustices of a banking system controlled by private wealth is that private money production does not exist in isolation. It is part of, and dependent on, the public infrastructure that makes up a nation's monetary, economic, taxation, legal and criminal justice systems.

In the first place, as explained above, all money is based on a currency, valued, authorised and issued by a country's central bank, and backed by taxpayers via their government. While some central banks may be deemed 'independent' of the government or public sector, in reality all central banks depend, for their power and authority, and for the value of the currency, on the support of taxpayers within their sovereign boundaries.

Central bankers also have different mandates. Some use their mandates to prioritise the interests of the private banking sector; the European Central Bank (ECB) is the most prominent in this regard. Others, like the Bank of England, support both the private banking sector, but also the government's economic objectives.

The most important role of any central bank is the determination and, if possible, maintenance of the value of a currency. The central bank's power to issue and maintain the value of a fiat currency is closely linked to the government's capacity to tax its citizens. In this sense fiscal policy acts as a vital backstop to monetary policy.

Central banks also play a critical role in managing the banking system as a whole, and in supporting private banks through lending and other operations. They exist in order to maintain financial stability for the economy as a whole. An important element of this support for the private sector is the bank rate or base rate, the interest rate charged to banks. Although the bank rate has an important influence on other lending rates in the real economy, it is used only by licensed commercial bankers and bears no direct relationship to the rates charged by these bankers on commercial loans. (Ask any small start-up business if they have ever been lucky enough to borrow money at the same rate as their banker paid to the central bank!) Invariably when there is public commentary about the central bank rate, the assumption is that all rates from commercial banks are as low as the bank rate. In fact, the variation on the bank rate can be very high for the full spectrum of lending, as any glimpse at advertised High Street real rates, those calculated to allow for inflation or deflation, will testify.

Money's stability and usefulness to both the wealthy and to the wider economy, therefore, depends on the sound maintenance of the currency's value, and on the public infrastructure that is the monetary and taxation system. In addition, the private banking system is heavily dependent on the taxpayer-backed public sector's judicial system to sustain and uphold, for example, private contracts. Enforceable contracts are fundamental to private money production, and to the accumulation of private wealth.

Individual financiers and institutions, such as AIG, that operate in international capital markets have since the Great Financial Crisis had their destabilising activities strongly backed by public, taxpayer-funded authorities. The nationalised Bank of England, the US Federal Reserve as well as the free-standing European Central Bank – all ultimately backed by taxpayers – have, since August 2007, provided the world's global banks and private financial markets with guarantees against losses, with historically low rates of interest on their borrowing, and with cheap and easy liquidity by way of monetary operations known as quantitative easing. (QE is the process whereby central banks purchase government debt or bonds from capital markets and place the bonds on their balance sheets. This cuts the number of bonds on the market, and because there is demand for 'safe' government bonds, the 'price' of these bonds rises, while simultaneously the 'yield' – comparable to the rate of interest – falls. This action helps bring down interest rates on government debt, but also on interest rates across the spectrum of lending.)

Actions by these public authorities mimic those in communist China or the old Soviet Union. All have, at different times, helped financial institutions avoid the discipline imposed by the 'free market' on risk-takers. In doing so, these public rescues have made a mockery of free market theory. Many financial institutions that operate as private firms in the global sphere are effectively nationalised institutions, thanks to this kind of public, central bank largesse.

Unfortunately, western democratic governments do not use existing powers to restrain the reckless conduct of international financiers and speculators. Instead, since the 1960s, elected governments have slowly and surreptitiously ceded even greater powers to global financial corporations to move capital offshore and across borders, and to create credit without oversight, regulation, taxation or restraint.

Unmanaged global capital mobility means sovereign nations have rendered their authorities powerless to tax or regulate capital flows. Instead democracies are effectively held to ransom by offshore capital and corporations, whose shareholders and owners demand the right to go further, and disregard national laws, values and institutions. The effective capture of the supine nation state by global bankers and financiers means that taxpayers are *obliged* to finance and maintain public legal and judicial systems in the service of such private wealth. We do that without any promise that offshore, mobile private wealth will reciprocate by contributing their fair share to the taxation system.

These tensions between private financial interests and society as a whole have throughout history been manifest in struggles for control over the money production system. Only intermittently has society succeeded in asserting democratic management of the system, by subordinating the interests of private wealth to wider interests. The Bretton Woods era (1945–71) was a time during which the private banking and finance sector acted as servant to and not master of the economy. Thanks largely to John Maynard Keynes's theories, his understanding of the monetary system, and to the implementation of his monetary policies during this period, the financial system was made to work largely in the interests of wider society.

However from the 1960s onwards, private wealth, led largely by private bankers, in collusion with elected politicians, began again to wrest control of the monetary system away from the regulatory democracy of governments. Today the global economy is effectively governed by a small number of actors based in private global banks and other financial institutions. They manage the system in their own vested interests to the detriment of wider society. In the absence of any real political challenge from society, private wealth owners have used the public infrastructure of money, and their power over private money production, to amass astounding amounts of wealth.

CHAPTER 3

The 'Price' of Money

The development of the credit system takes place as a reaction against usury. This violent fight against usury ... on the one hand robs usurer's capital of its monopoly by concentrating all fallow money reserves and throwing them on the money-market, and on the other hand limits the monopoly of the precious metals themselves by creating credit-money.

Karl Marx, Capital, Vol. III

Given there is no necessary limit to the volume of credit and debt that can be created by private, commercial banks, then credit is essentially *a free good* – not subject to finitude or to the market forces of supply and demand. From this it follows, as Keynes argued in his *Treatise on Money* but also in *The General Theory*, that 'the fee' or rate of interest on a loan, should always be low in real terms (i.e. taking account of inflation).

The development of monetary systems for the creation and management of credit was, as noted in an earlier chapter, a revolutionary advance for civilisation, simply because it ensured the wider availability of finance. That finance in turn generated economic activity, such as employment, creativity, innovation, scientific inquiry, the provision of goods and services – activity that society deemed useful or important. (Sometimes it financed wars, which society also deemed important). Economic activity and employment in turn generated income – wages, profits and tax revenues – the total of which far exceeded the banker's catalytic finance.

But just as important to society and the economy was the

impact this greater availability of finance had in lowering the 'price' of money, or the rate of interest.[1]

John Law, John Maynard Keynes, Karl Marx and other economists and historians recognised that once the system of bank money evolved, and credit became more widely available, society no longer needed to rely on existing wealth holders for finance. Robber barons in their castles – owners of surplus capital – were no longer sole providers of loan finance to the rest of the economy. They no longer had the power to hold borrowers to ransom. They could no longer argue that there was an 'opportunity cost' to the lender if he or she handed savings over to another, rather than investing it in a profitable enterprise. They could no longer argue that creditors had every right to demand a high rate of return. This argument no longer had force because savings were no longer needed to finance new ventures, new opportunities, new investment. The powers exercised in earlier times by the owners of wealth could be subordinated to society's wider interests. Credit creation by banks could now provide finance to those who needed funds for investment, and these bankers largely provided finance on the basis of the credibility of the borrower and the potential income to be gained from the enterprise; not on an arbitrary basis. Creative artists and designers, risk-taking entrepreneurs and innovators no longer had to pay usurious rates for finance to fund, for example, a scientific breakthrough or the staging of a new opera.

This was a very important development. The rate of interest on credit charged for economic activity is fundamental to the health and stability of an economy, because *the level of employment and activity in an economy depends critically on the rate of interest*. It is also important for ensuring that the credit is sustainable, and the debt repayment affordable, which is why much attention is paid to interest rates in this book. Rates that are too high stifle enterprise, creativity and initiative, and ultimately render debts unpayable.

The development of the monetary system as a reaction to usury

In periods that pre-dated monetary systems, it was the owners of pre-existing assets such as land (the creditors) that exercised huge power over those without assets but in need of money or credit (the borrowers). The moral dimension of this power relationship has, throughout history, led to the condemnation of usury – exploitative rates of interest – by faiths including Judaism, Islam and Christianity. For example, the principle of periodic debt cancellation to restore stability and social justice (the principle of Jubilee) was common to all three of the major faiths.

As Marx notes in the quotation at the beginning of this chapter, the development of the banking system and of a system of credit arose as a reaction to usury. Rates of interest, in particular usurious rates, can be used by those with wealth to effortlessly extract 'rent' or additional wealth from borrowers. Monetary systems evolved and developed in the seventeenth and eighteenth centuries as debtors and wider society eventually reacted against such exploitation.

The extraction of wealth from borrowers is compounded when payments to the lender, creditor or rentier are delayed or halted so that the lender can make exponential gains from debtors. As such, the practice of exploitative moneylending at high rates of interest is widely viewed as parasitical, with humanity and the ecosystem as host, and helps further stratify wealth and poverty. The rich effortlessly become richer, and the poor and indebted become ever more entrenched in their debt and impoverishment.

Christian leaders – until about the late sixteenth century – condemned usury, and punished bankers and other creditors with ostracism and excommunication. They were denied the chance to be buried in sacred ground or for their sons and daughters to be married in a church. Cosimo de Medici, the great Florentine banker, in a clear attempt to absolve himself and his heirs of any potential charge of usury by the Church, paid for the restoration of a monastery, among other investments, in return for a papal bull that redeemed him of past sins.

In time, Christianity's prohibition of usury was to be modified by John Calvin (1509–64) and other Christian leaders. On the four-hundredth anniversary of Calvin's birth the *Financial Times* noted that Calvin's escape from French Catholic rule, and his arrival in Geneva led to 'a huge influx of protestants from France, following in Calvin's footsteps [who] brought ... skills to Geneva while the lifting of the Catholic Church's ban on usury paved the way for the city's pre-eminence in private banking.'[2]

Even while some branches of Islamic finance circumvent the Koranic law, Islam has always upheld the Koran's prohibition of the taking or giving of interest, or *riba* – regardless of the purpose of the loan. Islamic finance, if practiced along the lines of the Koran, is largely 'stakeholder finance' with lenders sharing risks with borrowers. The *riba* prohibition includes the whole notion of effortless profit or earnings that arise without work or value-added production in commerce. In Islam money can only be lent and used for facilitating trade and commerce, not for the making of capital gains (or rent) on the money itself. Islamic scholars were fully aware that moneylending could stratify wealth, exacerbate exploitation, and lead to the eventual enslavement of those who do not own assets. Because Arabs were the world's foremost mathematicians, having imported the decimal system invented by Hindus, they fully understood the 'magical' qualities of compound interest, and its ability to multiply and magnify debts.

Usury is today widely accepted as normal in western economies whose monetary systems have been weakened by the parasitic grasp of finance capital, and enfeebled by heavy burdens of debt. This acceptance blinds society to the way in which usury exacerbates the destructive *extraction of assets from the earth*.

The 'Price' of Money

This happens because, as the English radiochemist, Professor Frederick Soddy (1877–1956) once explained,

> Debts are subject to the laws of mathematics rather than physics.
>
> Unlike wealth which is subject to the laws of thermodynamics, debts do not rot with old age and are not consumed in the process of living ... On the contrary (debts) grow at so much per cent per annum, by the well-known mathematical laws of simple and compound interest ... which leads to infinity ... a mathematical not a physical quantity.[3]

By contrast, earth and its assets are finite and subject to the process of decay. Nature's curve for growth is almost flat; the rate of interest's curve is linear. Compounded interest's curve is exponential, as the late Margrit Kennedy demonstrated in the chart below.[4]

In its earliest stages, 'easy but dear' credit fuels an expansion of speculation and consumption. Property and other

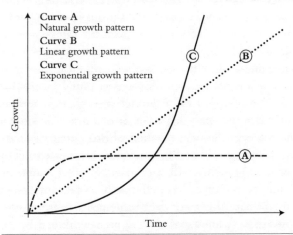

Source: This Time is Different: A Panoramic View of Eight Centuries of Financial Crises by Carmen M. Reinhart, University of Maryland and NBER; and Kenneth S. Rogoff, Harvard University and NBER.

Fig. 2. Illustrations of different growth patterns.

asset prices boom. Shopping malls become the temples of the High Street. But debts have to be repaid from income, whether the form of income comes as wages, salaries, profits or tax revenues. If rates of interest are too high, debtors have to raise the funds for debt repayment by increasing rates of profit, and by the further extraction of value.

These pressures to increase income at exponential rates for the repayment of debt implies that both labour and the land (defined broadly) have to be exploited at ever-rising rates. Those who labour by hand or brain work harder and longer to repay rising, real levels of mortgage or credit card debt. It is no accident therefore that the deregulation of finance led to the deregulation of working hours, and the abolition of Sunday as a day of rest. Instead, longer hours of work – '24/7' – with shops open 24 hours a day for 7 days a week – became an acceptable practice as the finance sector's values took precedence over other considerations.

The pressures on the earth's limited resources also rise in line with rent extraction. The world's seas have to be fished out, forests have to be stripped, and the 'productivity' of the land intensified – at the same compounded rate as interest rates. High-yield crops, the use of fertilisers and pesticides, the constraining of animals indoors, increases in food production not just for the world's growing population but to make food production *more profitable* – all this must be done in order to repay debt. The effects are well known: soil and sea degradation, salination of irrigated areas, over-extraction and pollution of groundwater, resistance to pesticides, erosion of biodiversity, and so on. In other words, the earth's limited resources have effectively to be cannibalised if the mathematical laws of debt repayments to the world's creditors are to be honoured.

It is not just workers who are hurt by finance capital's exploitation of their labour and the extraction of wealth by way of high rates on debt. Firms, entrepreneurs, hospital administrators, university chancellors, inventors and engineers, innovators and artists of all kinds find their efforts thwarted by bankers or 'private equity investors' demanding higher rates of rent, and a larger share of the returns on investment, creativity, skill, hard work and innovation. As this process snowballs, not only does the 'rent' on money rise, but rents for all sorts of activities rise.

The high real rates of the neoliberal era

As argued above, the supply of money or credit is without limit – and so must be managed. Its over-supply, and the tendency of creditors to lend pro-cyclically, should, if anything, suppress its price. Not so. Interest rates, in real terms, have risen steadily over the period since policies for the management of both bank lending standards and interest rates were abandoned. Indeed, high rates of interest have punctured credit bubbles with painful regularity since the 1970s.

The chart below, Figure 3, is one of very few that shows the progress of interest rates. It depicts in nominal terms (i.e. not adjusted for inflation) the official Bank of England Rate between 1914 and 2009. As central bank rates are on the whole lower than commercial bank rates, this is a guide that suggests what were the much higher rates for loans to individuals and firms. Take note of the period between 1933 and 1950 when policies for enforcing lending standards, and for applying Keynes's liquidity preference theories, were applied by Britain's authorities. Over this period both interest rates and inflation were subdued. Note also that as finance was liberalised, and the creation of too much credit chasing too few goods and services led to inflation, the central bank's rate rose too – both in line with inflation, but also as a symptom of the volatility caused by liberalisation. The central bank rate in turn pushed up rates in real terms for the full spectrum of loans in the real economy: short and long-term loans; safe and risky loans.

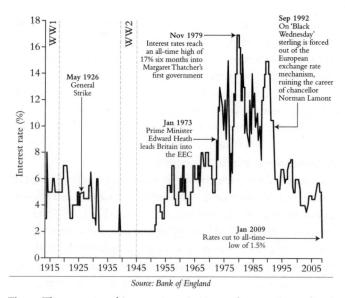

Fig. 3. The progress of interest rates in nominal terms. Reproduced with acknowledgements to the *Financial Times*.

Thatcherism and the return of 'robber barons'

The deregulation of credit creation began in the UK in 1971 with the launch of 'competition and credit control' (CCC), often described by economists as 'all competition and no control'. Duncan Needham, of the Cambridge University Centre for Financial History, has written at length on the subject, and argues that:

> CCC swept away the restrictions on ... bank lending to the private sector, that had been in place for much of the 1960s. Henceforth, bank lending would be controlled on the basis of cost, that is, through interest rates. Loans would be granted to those companies and individuals that could pay the highest rate rather than those that fulfilled the authorities' qualitative criteria. By allocating bank credit competitively 'on the basis of cost', CCC replaced years of credit rationing 'by control'.[5]

CCC was not a success. While it aimed to control 'the money supply', the effect was the opposite. The money supply grew by 72 percent before the policy was abandoned, and two years later inflation peaked at 26.9 percent.

First, British and then other western central bankers relinquished rationing and control over lending standards, and over the full spectrum of lending rates: short and long rates, safe and risky rates and rates in real (allowing for inflation) terms. Finance capital – the robber barons of our day – had regained power over the financial system, and once again exercised control over the pricing of loans and over decisions about who would get loans, that is, the eligibility of companies and individuals. If borrowers could not afford the highest rates (because, for example, the highest rates exceeded the rate of profit on an enterprise) then loans would not be made. However, if borrowers were willing to bear almost all the risk of high real rates of interest, bankers dished out credit liberally. In this way, private bankers were once again freed up to create 'easy' (unregulated) credit, often for the purpose of speculation. The inevitable happened: between 1971 and 1974 credit expansion fuelled consumption and led to a 35 percent rise in consumer prices, and to a fall in sterling. Import prices rose by 79 percent, and wages tried to keep up. Loss of control over bank lending was a key factor, and the simultaneous switch to flexible exchange rates was another.[6]

Second, as private bankers were freed up to fix rates on that 'easy money' for speculative activity, so interest rates were steadily ratcheted upwards, as Figure 3 shows. For the next thirty years, high real rates periodically bankrupted many fine individuals, firms, industries and economies.

Thatcherism culminates in 2007–09 crash
The root cause of the crisis that led to the bankruptcy of Lehman's and other banks in 2008 was the bursting of a vast bubble of *unaffordable* credit.

Very few economists blame the cause of the crisis on 'easy' – i.e. poorly regulated and costly – credit creation. Many regard 'easy' credit as 'cheap' credit, but easy credit can be dear. That is, unregulated credit (offered, for example, to sub-prime borrowers, or for 'liar loans') can be fixed at very high real rates of interest. Easy credit can also, of course, be cheap. The alternative to easy credit is 'tight' credit, meaning credit creation that is carefully regulated and only offered to firms, individuals or for projects that can expect to generate sound potential income flows. According to Keynes, the best form of credit creation is 'tight, but cheap' credit.

Few economists propose increased regulation of credit creation and interest rates. Most focus on the low rates that prevailed after the bursting of the 2001 dotcom bubble, and explain low rates as *causal* of the crisis. However, these

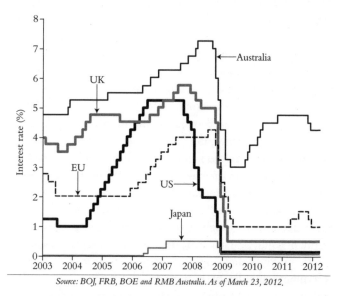

Source: BOJ, FRB, BOE and RMB Australia. As of March 23, 2012.

Fig. 4. Chart taken from the presentation by Richard Koo, Chief Economist, Nomura Research Institute, Tokyo, to the INET Conference, Berlin, 14 April 2012.

rates were set low as *a reaction* to the bursting of that asset bubble. And while it is true that post-2001 low rates laid the ground for the next crisis, they were not the immediate cause. Vast amounts of easy, dear money unrelated to real economic activity, triggered the crisis. It was easy credit that blew up the credit bubble, including variations on 'liar loans' or 'no-documentation mortgages', or the packaged and re-packaged pools of mortgages sliced and diced into securities by banks like Goldman Sachs. The risks on these were then sold and cynically passed on to the 'little people' – borrowers and shareholders – as well as to big institutional investors.

Nor do most mainstream economists give proper weight to the steady rise in interest rates after 2003–04, and the impact of rising rates on already over-indebted firms, households and individuals. Figure 4, from the economist Richard Koo, shows just how sharp these rises were in the run up to the crisis.

It was higher interest rates that, like a dagger pointed at a balloon, burst the credit/asset price bubble that precipitated the crash of 2007–09.

At the height of the credit boom, as late as 2005–07, loans or mortgages were still being offered to individuals, households and firms without any real assessment by bankers of the ability to repay. Some of these borrowers were high-risk (e.g. 'sub-prime') borrowers, and could therefore be milked for usurious rates of interest. The returns on these loans were scandalously high, which is why banks like Goldman Sachs demanded of their bank agents that they arrange more of such lending. They gathered up these sub-prime mortgages, bundled them up and artificially *created new assets* – a mixed bundle of mortgages and loans – they called 'collateralised debt obligations' or CDOs. These new financial products or assets could be sold again, or bet against for massive capital gains. They could also be transformed into new assets and used as collateral to back up (lever-age) additional new borrowing *by bankers*. That is, until the individuals, households and firms at the heart of the CDOs defaulted, the debt bubble popped, and the 'sub-prime' crisis erupted.

To imagine the role that sub-prime debt played in the crisis, it helps to think of sub-primers as positioned at the base of a vast, upside-down pyramid of debt. Although their debts were not substantial in the grand scheme of things, nevertheless they were the poorest, most vulnerable borrow-ers in the market – and because they were charged the highest rates, were most likely the first to go under. Balanced precari-ously above sub-prime debts were huge sums of 'structured' and often 'synthetic' debt, made up of collateralised securities, credit default swaps and other complex financial products. These financially engineered products, created artificially by the shadow banking system in the run-up to the crisis, were explosive precisely because they bore no relation to the real world of productive activity. However, they were tenu-ously linked to the properties and mortgages – the assets – of poor workers.

It took only the default of some of the poorest borrowers at the bottom of the financial pyramid to blow up the entire global financial system. This was an extraordinary develop-ment; one in which the debts of the poorest in society caused a systemic crisis for the richest. Costas Lapavistas writes that 'under conditions of classical, nineteenth-century capitalism it would have been unthinkable for a global disruption of accumulation to materialize because of debts incurred by workers, including the poorest.'[7]

Little has been done since the 2007–09 crisis to remove control over rates of interest from commercial bankers. Despite falls in central bank rates since then, commercial bankers continue to set and determine high real rates on loans and overdrafts for individuals, households and firms in the real economy. Journalists and other commentators mistakenly continue to couple central bank rates with commercial rates, as if low rates apply across the board. But they are not equivalent. Very few entrepreneurs can borrow for new investments at the Bank of England's (current) inter-bank rate of 0.5 percent, or the ECB's benchmark rate which at the time of writing (April 2016) is 0.0 percent. Only banks or financial institutions registered with the central bank enjoy the benefit of that policy rate. The rates on loans made to firms and individuals are determined – socially constructed – by those engaged in the creation of loans: commercial bankers. Bankers make decisions about the rate of interest on a loan based on their assessment of the riskiness of the borrower, and on the rate of return they seek for themselves, but also on what other creditors are offering borrowers in the market place. Given that the banking sector is oligopolistic, there is in reality very little competition and instead a great deal of collusion on decisions about rates.

How rates are 'fixed' by private, commercial bankers

The LIBOR – London Interbank Offered Rate – is critical to determining the rate of interest on $800 trillion–worth of global financial instruments, including millions of mortgages. In 2008 the *Wall Street Journal* began drawing attention to the manipulation of LIBOR. The scandal erupted in 2012 and brought to the attention of the general public, but also to economists and regulatory authorities, the role played by the British Bankers Association (a cartel) and back office bank staff – the 'submitters' – in 'fixing' the price of inter-bank loans. The exposure of this fraud suddenly made clear that these rates were not determined by the 'invisible hand', the demand for or supply of money. Instead, the rate was fixed by back office staff determined to make money for the bank and to ensure their annual bonus exceeded the last year's bonus. *The Economist* examined 'The Rotten Heart of Finance':

The most memorable incidents in earth-changing events are sometimes the most banal. In the rapidly spreading scandal of LIBOR (the London Interbank Offered Rate) it is the very everydayness with which bank traders set about manipulating the most important figure in finance. They joked, or offered small favours. 'Coffees will be coming your way,' promised one trader in exchange for a fiddled number. 'Dude. I owe you big time! ... I'm opening a bottle of Bollinger,' wrote another. One trader posted diary notes to himself so that he wouldn't forget to fiddle the numbers the next week. 'Ask for High 6M Fix', he entered in his calendar, as he might have put 'Buy Milk'.

What may still seem to many to be a parochial affair involving Barclays, a 300-year-old British bank, rigging an obscure number, is beginning to assume global significance. The number that the traders were toying with determines the prices that people and corporations around the world pay for loans or receive for their savings. It is used as a benchmark to set payments on about $800 trillion–worth of financial instruments, ranging from complex interest-rate derivatives to simple mortgages. The number determines the global flow of billions of dollars each year. Yet it turns out to have been flawed.[8]

How the authorities can influence rates

For it [loanable funds] is concerned with changes in the demand for bank borrowing, whereas I am concerned with changes in the demand for money; and those who desire to hold money only overlap partially and temporarily with those who desire to be in debt to the banks.

John Maynard Keynes, *Collected Writings XIV*

Keynes's 'liquidity preference theory' outlined in *The General Theory of Employment, Interest and Money* provided central bankers and governments not just with an understanding of how interest rates are determined but also with policies for managing and keeping rates of interest low across the full spectrum of lending during the Second World War and beyond.[9] This was a time when Britain's government borrowed more than it had ever borrowed before and public debt peaked at 250 percent of GDP – yet interest rates remained relatively low across the board. Geoff Tily in *Keynes Betrayed* writes:

> Liquidity preference theory led [Keynes] to conclusions of the most profound importance. Ultimately, the theory turned classical analysis on its head. The rate of interest was the cause, argued Keynes, not the passive consequence, of the level of economic activity and in particular, of the level of employment.[10]

Yet this revolutionary monetary theory and its associated policies are largely ignored by the economics profession, and forgotten by regulators and policy-makers.

Central to Keynes's theory is an understanding of bank money not just as a means of creating purchasing power for the purposes of exchange, but also as a store of value. When, after borrowing and investing, the holder of borrowed money makes profits or capital gains, she will face decisions about what to do with her surplus. Keynes argued that, like other holders of capital, her decision about where to place and for how long to hold her savings is determined first by a need for *cash*, for immediate or near-immediate use in purchasing goods and services (i.e. short-term 'liquidity'); second, by what he called the precautionary motive: the desire for *security* as to the future equivalent of her cash; and third, by the speculative motive: the desire to secure *gains* by investing the money in projects and knowing better than the market what the future will bring.

The creation of bank money within a developed monetary system, as explained in earlier chapters, means that those fortunate enough to build up a surplus of capital *are no longer sole providers of loan finance* to the rest of the economy; nor indeed do they determine rates of interest. There is no need for these owners of capital to share their wealth by lending to others active in the economy and neither in these circumstances should they have control over lending rates. The business of lending can then be confined to a carefully regulated banking sector. As a result, owners of surplus capital can be forced to play a more passive role by deploying their capital in more economically useful outlets. When they are held at bay by society in this way, capitalists are obliged to find different outlets for the investment of their surpluses.

Keynes concluded therefore that the rate of interest can be influenced not by a demand for *savings* (as monetarists argue) but by a demand for *safe or risky assets*, with the saver's money invested in those assets for different motives and over different periods of time. By issuing and managing a full range of such assets (in particular safe and valuable government bonds) government treasuries working with central banks can jointly create and manage a full range of assets needed by investors to satisfy their cash, security and capital gains (speculative) motives. By dominating the markets for these assets, the central bank and treasury can thereby influence and manage the spectrum of interest rates applied across the economy for loans of different maturities and risk.

Unsurprisingly, these policies did not appeal to the robber barons of the day. Such monetary policies undermined their power over the economy, and marginalised their role in setting interest rates. So, almost immediately after the Second World War, the finance sector recruited (directly or indirectly) economists, journalists and politicians to reverse Keynes's monetary theories and policies, and to denounce him as a 'tax and spender'. This, despite the fact that Keynes was concerned overwhelmingly with the management of monetary policy for the purpose of maintaining employment and activity. He considered that when in a crisis the need arose to deploy fiscal policy, it was invariably a sign of monetary policy failure.

The intellectual coup against Keynes's ideas and policies, most of which took place at the London School of Economics and included some of Keynes's so-called disciples, led ultimately to the victory of the economy's robber barons. As a long-term consequence both of that coup but also of the return of orthodox economics, the interests of the world's people, but also of the ecosystem, is once again subordinated to the interests of global finance. Central bankers and government treasuries no longer even try to manage the full spectrum of interest rates, nor do they offer a sufficient range of safe assets as alternatives to those available in the private sector. Those with savings who wish to invest for the *security motive* (for example, pension funds) currently struggle vainly to find safe assets in which to park investments for the long-term. Among the safest assets are US government bonds (US 'treasuries') and British government bonds ('gilts'). Unfortunately the slump of 2007–09 and its aftermath cut government tax revenues dramatically, as firms failed, individuals lost employment and wages fell in real terms. Instead of supporting the heavily indebted private sector by expanding public investment, increasing employment and supporting wages after the crisis, western governments responded to the slump by cutting spending further. This meant that governments stopped borrowing, and the issue of government bonds declined. At about the same time, central banks embarked on quantitative easing and, by purchasing government bonds and placing them on their balance sheets, helped create a shortage of such safe assets. As a consequence, the prices of all assets have risen, including government bonds, and the yields (the return an investor will realize on a bond) have fallen – in some cases to negative levels!

Because of these low yields (returns) and this shortage of bonds, capitalists have to park their funds in other assets.

The most attractive asset is property: valuable and scarce real estate in, for example, inner London, New York City or Hong Kong. The outcome of low yields on government bonds is the massive inflation of property prices – which in turn has led to a form of 'social cleansing' as prices rocket and ordinary Londoners, for example, can no longer afford to purchase property or pay high rents.

Pensioners dependent on their savings for income similarly go in search of assets that will generate sufficient income to keep pace with inflation. As a result, savings and surpluses are poured into a small group of assets regarded as safe by investors, including, gold, jewels, stocks and shares, and government bonds. This has led, predictably, to the inflation of these assets as well. As it is the rich who on the whole own assets (i.e. stocks and shares, but also football clubs, public hospital car parks, land, brands, race-horses, works of art, yachts, etc), the rich have grown richer. And as the value of their assets has risen, so have the rents they charge on those assets.

Nothing better explains the rise in inequality than this process.

Central bankers appear helpless to deal with asset price inflation – only because they have abandoned Keynes's advice of how central banks and governments can work together to intervene, to manage both the production of a range of assets needed by investors and the pricing or the rate of interest on those assets. Instead the determination of interest rates for the economy as a whole remains, still, in the hands of the private sector's 'invisible hand' – global finance capital.

The rate of interest as weapon

Wielding the weapon of interest, finance capital effectively holds societies, governments and industries, but also the entire ecosystem, to ransom over repayment of its loans. This predicament is particularly tragic given that, in theory, the development of banking and of sound monetary systems should have ended the power of any elite to extract outsized returns from borrowers. Today, just as in earlier pre-banking eras, interest rates remain high in real terms, even in rich countries. However, this is only because these societies, elected governments and industries have conceded such despotic power to finance capital.

CHAPTER 4

The Mess We're In

We live in turbulent political and financial times, and in a global economy dogged by failure. We survive precariously on a planet warmed by human greenhouse gas emissions and disturbed by a human-induced mass extinction. The financial system is currently volatile, corrupted and widely discredited. Scandals of mis-selling, theft, manipulation and fraud abound. And the cry 'there is no money' for projects that society holds dear echoes all around us. We are assured that 'there is no money' for care of the elderly, or for the mentally ill, or for social housing. There is no money for the commissioning of operas, plays or other forms of artistic creation. There is no money for public investment in water conservation, renewable energy, flood defences, the retrofitting of old, energy-leaking properties, or other investments designed to protect society from climate change.

One of the reasons for this chorus of defeatism is the global overhang of debt, and the conflation by many economists (and indeed the public) of both public and private debt. In this chapter I hope to deal with both the 'there is no money' meme, and the differences between public and private debt, and why public debt, at times of weakness, ought not to be a barrier to public investment.

'The state has no source of money'
At the heart of the politically inept responses to the financial crisis is an ideologically driven and mendacious conviction: that while society can afford to bail out a systemically broken banking system, it cannot afford to finance and address

economic failure, youth unemployment, energy insecurity, climate change, poverty and disease. Society, it is argued, 'has no money' to finance these challenges, to stimulate recovery or create employment.

Mrs Thatcher, whose views on the economy still inform the policies of many conservative and social democratic governments, gave clearest expression to the conviction that 'there is no money' in a 1983 speech:

> The state has no source of money, other than the money people earn themselves. If the state wishes to spend more it can only do so by borrowing your savings, or by taxing you more. And it's no good thinking that someone else will pay. That someone else is you.
>
> There is no such thing as public money. There is only tax-payers' money.[1]

Today this assertion sits strangely with the facts of the recent bailout of the global banking system. While politicians try to persuade electorates that 'there is no money', something quite different happened under the guise of quantitative easing. Central bankers created trillions of dollars 'out of thin air' and did so essentially overnight to bail out the banking system.

And I mean trillions.

The American senator Bernie Sanders directed the US Government Accountability Office to undertake an audit of the amount of 'state money' created by the US Federal Reserve and supported by governments during the crisis. The conclusion was that $16 trillion 'in total financial assistance' had been mobilised for 'some of the largest financial institutions and corporations in the United States and throughout the world'.[2] Please note that not a cent of these trillions of dollars was raised by taxing Americans, although the liquidity created by the Federal Reserve *is* backed by US taxpayers.

Second, note that the beneficiaries of all this American tax-payer-backed largesse included German, British and French bankers.

Here in Britain, the governor of the Bank of England explained to a Scottish conference in October 2009 that 'a trillion (that is, one thousand billion) pounds, close to two-thirds of the annual output of the entire (British) economy', had been mobilised (again, almost overnight) to bail out the British banking system.[3] 'Never in the field of financial endeavour ... has so much money been owed by so few to so many.'[4]

Despite this evidence that the state does indeed have 'other sources of money' – other, that is, than taxation – many have adopted Mrs Thatcher's reasoning, including those on the progressive end of the political spectrum:

'Dear Chief Secretary, I'm afraid to tell you there's no money left,' wrote Liam Byrne, a British labour treasury minister, in a letter to his successor published in the *Guardian* on 17 May 2010.[5]

'The British government has run out of money because all the money was spent in the good years', said George Osborne, Britain's chancellor of the exchequer, on Sky News on 27 February 2012.[6]

'We will have to govern with much less money around,' noted Ed Balls, Britain's opposition chancellor, in a speech 'Striking the Right Balance for the British Economy', delivered at Thomson Reuters on 3 June 2013.[7]

Austerity – because 'there is no money'

The political mantra 'there is no money' is designed to explain the need for austerity and other unpalatable policies. Austerity, in turn, is a policy used by politicians as an opportunity created by the crisis to cut public spending and shrink the state. This was confirmed by the economist Jeremy Warner, deputy editor of the UK's *Daily Telegraph* who wrote that

> In the end, you are either a big-state person or a small-state person, and what big-state people hate about austerity is that its primary purpose is to shrink the size of government spending ...
>
> The bottom line is that you can only really make serious inroads into the size of the state during an economic crisis. This may be pro-cyclical, but there is never any appetite for it in the good times; it can only be done in the bad.[8]

In adopting austerity policies politicians have effectively resorted to the very dated 'gold standard' policies of the 1920s and '30s. Just as then, they have once again imposed or tolerated contractionary and deflationary policies on whole populations in Europe, Japan and the US. Contractionary policies have the effect of lowering the money supply and, with it, profits, wages, incomes and prices.

At the same time, the deflation brought on by economic contraction has led to a rise, not a fall, in public debt.

Unlike inflation which erodes the value of debt, deflationary pressures increase the cost and value of debt. Debt is defined as an asset by its owners: creditors and international financiers, including private equity investors. Assets are valuable in themselves – think of the rent extracted from property, from income streams generated by the purchase of a football club, or from companies in the form of dividends, etc. But debt (or a loan) is also an asset and has value as a source of 'rent' in the form of interest payments made over time. Finally, debts (for example, a bank's mortgages) are useful as income-generating collateral for leveraging even more borrowing or debt. Think of phone network providers that have thousands of contracts with users. These contracts represent streams of revenue into the future, and holding these contracts provides the phone network company with the collateral needed against further borrowing.

Deflationary policies and pressures are welcome to asset-holders, bankers and creditors: they cause the value of debt and other financial assets to rise relative to prices and incomes. (Of course they often blithely ignore the fact that policies which increase the cost of debt while lowering the incomes of debtors mean that these debtors may default on their obligations.)

At the same time deflationary pressures raise the value of cash because *the real value of money rises*. In a credit-based economy with an overhang of debt, the fall in lending or borrowing leads to a fall in the money supply. This shortage of money or cash, causes the real value of cash to rise. Secondly, in a debt-deflationary environment when holders of debt cannot transform their liabilities into cash, cash becomes king. In 1930s New York, when deflation caused the cost of debt and interest rates to rise, those mortgaged to the hilt could not sell their properties because of a lack of buyers. The prices of properties plummeted, and those with cash and few debts were able to snap them up at rock-bottom prices.

Contractionary austerity policies shrink *public* investment at the very time when the *private* sector is over-indebted, weak, lacks confidence in the future and has slashed investment. By cutting public investment in a period of private sector weakness, governments curtail not just public sector activities but also private sector activity, profits, wages, incomes and tax revenues. As such, austerity serves to exacerbate the indebtedness, 'the overhang of private debt', of western firms, households and individuals as well as that of states. Austerity effectively punishes those *innocent* of causing the crisis – those dependent on state welfare – while deflationary pressures increase the value of assets owned by those *responsible* for the crisis. For a few years after the bankruptcy of Lehman Brothers, rising debt levels were made bearable by the low rates of interest that were a *reaction* to the 2007–09 crisis. However, as noted earlier, central banks can only strongly influence the base or policy rate, and loans at this rate are only available to banks and financial institutions. Commercial interest rates remained high in real terms, that is, relative to deflating prices and wages.

However, rates were expected to rise even further if and when central bank rates rose. Rises in rates on longer-term assets (bonds and mortgages) would have a punitive impact on heavily indebted firms and households, not to mention governments. This explains why in 2016 central bankers were so reluctant to raise their 'benchmark' rates in case the ripple effect on other rates bankrupted the economy. Indeed, each time there were signs of the US or UK economy improving, recovery was choked off by either the threat, or the reality, of rising bond yields (rates) in global capital markets.

Financial crises, austerity and disillusionment with democracy

The politicians responsible for enforcing austerity policies had not just imposed unnecessary suffering and dislocation on millions of people, their communities and countries. They had not only caused public debt to rise. They, in fact, caused disillusionment with democracy to set in among the unemployed and impoverished in Europe and the US. Austerity and the collusion between politicians and the finance sector opened up political space for right-wing, populist political parties like Donald Trump and the Tea Party in the US, the National Front in France, and Golden Dawn in Greece. These were among the social and political consequences of democratic politicians enacting policies that enrich the few while impoverishing the majority; policies based on the interests of the robber barons and on the flawed theories of 'defunct' economists.

As this goes to press, almost nine years have passed since the 'credit crunch' of August 2007. Yet the global economy struggled to recover from that crisis and the easy

66

(unregulated) credit-fuelled bubbles that were violently burst by rising real rates of interest. Instead of recovery, the crisis simply rolled around the global economy. It was at its most intense at the core – the US and the UK – but subsequently moved across to Europe and in particular the Eurozone. Then the crisis moved to emerging markets, and China in particular. Western economies experienced the longest period of economic failure in peacetime history. Only during periods of war was economic failure so prolonged. And yet, far from trying to correct imbalances by re-regulating the financial system, governments stood idly by as the global credit bubble – never fully deflated after 2008 – was reinflated by central bank operations such as quantitative easing. Having done little to re-structure or re-regulate the global finance sector, central bankers instead chose to use a range of monetary tools at their disposal to help bankers clean up their balance sheets. Commercial bankers drew on QE and other forms of cheap finance and, because they were not restrained by public authorities, used these resources for speculation – that is to say, gambling or betting:

> Many ideas central to financial mathematics began with betting … The scientists who cracked blackjack and roulette in the 1960s and '70s eventually moved into finance, tired of the attention from casino security. To them, the divide was superficial. Like the modern teams tackling sports betting, they just saw another market, another set of inefficiencies, and another game to be beaten.[9]

Speculation, especially the kind that tires of 'the attention of casino security' leads to quick and sometimes exponential gains for bankers and other financiers. These gains were invested in the ever-rising value of assets owned by wealthy financial elites. Commercial bankers did not, on the whole, ensure that these publicly financed resources were channelled into the real economy at affordable rates of interest. As a result, in major western economies, and increasingly in emerging market economies, the money supply was shrunk, investment, employment, wages and salaries fell, and the poor and unemployed were even more impoverished.

Prime Minister David Cameron declared in a speech at Davos in 2012, when the crisis had not yet receded, that while his government 'may be fiscal conservatives, we are monetary radicals injecting cash into the banking system'. This focus on the limited levers of monetary policy alone provided extraordinary comfort to, and wealth for, the finance sector, but failed to conjure up recovery. With the finance sector effectively insolvent, and industry both lacking in confidence and anyway too indebted to take investment risks, monetary policy *had* to work in tandem with fiscal policy, to help revive the economy, as the OECD argued in 2016: 'A stronger collective policy response is needed to strengthen demand. Monetary policy cannot work alone. Fiscal policy is now contractionary in many major economies. Structural reform momentum has slowed. All three levers of policy must be deployed more actively to create stronger and sustained growth.'[10]

Unfortunately, this message – echoed by other global financial institutions including central banks and the IMF – fell on deaf ears.

Economic recovery and bank lending could not be revived by fiscal conservatism and monetary radicalism. There could be no recovery when there were too few *private* borrowers active in the real economy as a result of the ongoing financial crisis. Potential and sound private borrowers were, and are, a rare breed in economies with high unemployment or part-time employment, falling wages, and rising insecurity. To compound the ongoing crises caused by the dearth of private borrowers and the shrinking money supply, orthodox economists. including some at bailed-out private banks, discouraged borrowing by the only remaining viable borrower – the government. They did this because of the flawed and intellectually dishonest notion that public borrowing would 'crowd out' private finance.

Richard Koo, an economist best known for his work on Japan's prolonged deflationary era, explained that QE did not work in Japan because of the absence of both private and public borrowers: 'If there were many willing borrowers and few able lenders, the Bank of Japan, as the ultimate supplier of funds, would indeed have to do something. *But when there are no borrowers the bank is powerless.*'[11]

The public sector: the borrower of last resort

How to create more borrowers, increase the money supply and with it economic recovery? The borrower of last resort – the government – *has* to intervene. It can do so by issuing gilts in the UK, or treasury bills in the US, and use the finance raised to invest and spend on productive, sustainable activities that create employment. Employment (as we all know from direct experience) generates income. If it is regular employment, it also generates tax revenues – with which to repay the debt. Public investment will, in a slump or at times of economic weakness, raise confidence, provide opportunities for the private sector, and by way of 'the multiplier' – explained below – simultaneously generate income for the government via increased tax revenues and reduced welfare payments.

Rising tax revenues from expanded, well-paid and skilled employment will reduce public debt as sure as night follows day.

The magic of the multiplier

The multiplier is an economic concept no longer generally recognised as valid by orthodox economists.[12] It is difficult not to conclude that the reason for this neglect may be that the multiplier operates as a direct result of public borrowing and investment, and orthodox economists are ideologically opposed to public borrowing and investment. However, in a welcome intervention, the IMF's chief economist recently startled the profession by reviving debate about the role of the multiplier – albeit the IMF's focus was on the *negative* impact of a *negative* multiplier.[13]

There can be no denying it: the multiplier has a critical impact on the economy. New spending financed by public borrowing has a series of repercussions that ripple through the economy. Thanks to the multiplier, the aggregate impact of public spending can be far larger than the catalytic jolt of the original government borrowing and expenditure. So the direct effects of government borrowing and investment on, say, a wind farm will first benefit the companies that produce the relevant wind farm equipment, their existing employees, and those who benefit from the new jobs created by investment in that industry. But the increase of employment doesn't stop there. There will also be a number of secondary repercussions. The extra wages and other incomes paid out will be invariably spent on extra purchases, which in turn leads to further employment. So the workers on the wind farm will shop for housing, food, transport, visits to the cinema, clothing and so on. 'If the resources of the country were already fully employed, these additional purchases would be mainly reflected in higher prices and increased imports', wrote Keynes. But in circumstances of weakness this would be true of only a small proportion of the additional consumption, since the greater part of it could be provided by already existing 'home' resources at present unemployed.[14]

These cumulative repercussions, triggered by the multiplier, are a virtuous reverse of the vicious downward cycle – the negative multiplier – brought on by financial failure and the contraction of economic activity caused by austerity.

Taxpayer backing for the private banking system

The reason why governments can borrow, even when public debt is high and the economy in recession, is explained by the relationship between a government and its central bank. Central banks are able to create large amounts of liquidity for both the government and the banking system at times of crisis *because* they are state institutions backed by taxpayers. Central banks, unlike private banks or firms or households, do not face solvency constraints. They are part of the government of a nation, and nations and their governments cannot be 'liquidated' in the way that a bankrupt firm can. (Some would say that Germany was 'liquidated' after the Second World War, in the sense that her financial and banking institutions were destroyed. However, as we all know, Germany remains a powerful nation and was able to rebuild her monetary and governmental institutions. Similarly, while Zimbabwe's economy is moribund, the nation and government of Zimbabwe continue to exist and to function. It is in this sense that nations and governments are different from entities such as firms.)

Of course sovereigns can *default* on debt repayments and can inflate debt away by printing too much money relative to economic activity – but that is not the same as 'liquidation' or bankruptcy of a sovereign.

In a crisis or a slump, a *sovereign* state can always call on or demand that both its central bank – the issuer of the currency – and also private or nationalised banks (such as the UK's RBS bank) should create money or credit in domestic currency. These funds can be used to finance, for example, private bank bailouts or government spending. Central banks cannot create money in foreign currencies, and so foreign debt becomes a significantly more challenging repayment burden than domestic debt.

The government's ability to raise finance in this way at low rates of interest is what distinguishes public finances from private finances. And while it is the case that governments can lose the confidence of investors, including foreign investors, this is most often the case because of economic weakness. Investors will lend to governments willing to invest in, maintain and expand the economic health of a nation. We have witnessed this over and over again as sovereign governments, like Russia after the 1998 default or Argentina in 2016, immediately attracted foreign funds. They did so for the simple reason that investors had confidence that the government would improve the economy, and that they, the investors, would benefit from the tax revenues generated by recovery.

Governments that run sound taxation systems can raise finance at low rates of interest because of that advantage over companies: the presence of an endless queue of economically active taxpayers, a queue that stretches forward into future generations. Which is why government borrowing should be, as far as possible, for the long-term benefit of society. Private firms are not guaranteed an endless stream of customers into the future; while firms or banks may expect future income streams from borrowers or rent-payers, these flows are not as certain as 'death and taxes'. If sound tax collection systems are in place, governments can generate the revenue needed to repay debts over future generations – which is why investors are keen to lend to sound sovereigns, and why sovereign debt, even during a recession, is favoured by international investors and largely considered safe.

As this book goes to press, with deflationary pressures bearing down on the economy, US equity investors have funneled $60 billion out of stock markets since the beginning of 2016 and, according to the *Financial Times*, 'sought the safety of cash, government debt and gold as sentiment continued to sour'.[15]

Commercial banking's failure to lend

Despite the injection of a massive increase in the supply of reserves and other financial resources by central banks, and despite the strengthening of their balance sheets, commercial banks have, for the reasons outlined above, continued to fail in their role as major co-creators of the money supply. The global banking system has not been fixed, re-structured or re-regulated after the crisis of 2007–09. Private debts in the Anglo-Saxon economies had not, on the whole, been paid down, deleveraged or re-structured (that is, rescheduled or written off). The global overhang of vast amounts of private debt remained a major barrier to recovery. A large proportion of this global debt was owed both to and by the private banking system, and was 'non-performing'.

An American analyst, Hoisington, points out that in 2015 US corporate debt increased by \$793 billion while total gross private domestic investment (which includes fixed and inventory investment) rose by a mere \$93 billion.[16] This suggests that the \$700 billion difference was used for unproductive, speculative activities. At the same time, corporate cash flow declined by \$224 billion and corporate profits fell by 15 percent to \$242.8 billion, their lowest level since the first quarter of 2011.

Central bank officials, politicians and the finance sector

As a result of austerity and the repression of lending by banks, citizens of the US and Europe endured years of suffering from rising unemployment, rents and taxes with falling incomes. Unemployment was higher, for example, in Spain than during the Great Depression. In the US very large numbers of workers had simply despaired and dropped out of the workforce, so their numbers did not appear in unemployment statistics. At the same time, ideologically driven governments used the opportunity of the crisis to cut back on welfare payments and to privatise public services.

Financial institutions fared better: they had privileged access to loans from central banks at very low or negative rates of interest. As noted above, bankers used 'easy' and cheap central bank liquidity to cover their losses, to borrow for speculative purposes, and to blow up new bubbles in a range of asset classes (property, bonds, stocks, commodities, etc.). By borrowing cheap from the central bank and lending dear into the real economy, private bankers were able, with the help of public servants at central banks, to re-capitalise their institutions and to clean up their balance sheets. These repairs to the finance sector's own finances were made at great cost to society and to the productive economy as a whole.

Because regulators and policy-makers had taken a hands off approach to the private banking system, the public authorities (both political and official) could not, and did not, ensure that finance was transmitted to the rest of the economy. Central bankers, politicians and regulators baulked at nationalising or re-regulating banks. Even when banks were nationalised, regulators did not use taxpayer-funded bailouts to require terms and conditions from bankers that would result in better management of credit creation and a more effective financial transmission system. They seemed unable to learn from the 1930s, when governments did impose conditions on private bankers, and so regained control over the financial system, and when central bankers did insist that private bankers adopt their 'guidance' on credit creation.

Nor did the world's politicians have the political will to regulate and stabilise the mobile, footloose flows of 'offshore' capital controlled by the private, and often corrupt, global banking system.

Partly because of this regulatory spinelessness, and in spite of a broken transmission system, the finance sector enjoyed 'business better than usual'. Although bankers and financiers may have faced solvency questions, they had been told that their institutions were too big to fail and they themselves too

'too big to jail', as US Attorney General Eric Holder said in evidence to a Congressional committee on 6 March 2013:

> I am concerned that the size of some of these institutions becomes so large that it does become difficult for us to prosecute them when we are hit with indications that if we do prosecute – if we do bring a criminal charge – it will have a negative impact on the national economy, perhaps even the world economy. I think that is a function of the fact that some of these institutions have become too large.[17]

As long as the banks remain vastly complex bundles of businesses, the executives running them remained above the law. No wonder they lobbied hard to prevent meaningful restructuring! Despite a supposed commitment to the ideology of 'free markets', market forces no longer imposed any meaningful constraints on the risks that a handful of very large banks had taken on. Instead, private financial institutions enjoyed taxpayer-backed protection – the very inverse of today's dominant and orthodox free market economic theory. This made bankers both parasitic on the state and dangerous for taxpayers, given that many continued to question the solvency of the world's biggest commercial banks. The *Financial Times* columnist Wolfgang Münchau used a 'back of an envelope' calculation to assess the extent to which banks are bust:

> The total balance sheet of the monetary and financial sector in the Eurozone stood at €26.7tn in April [2013] this year. How much of this is underwater? In Ireland, the ten largest banks accounted for losses of 10 percent of total banking assets in that country. The total loss will be higher. In Greece, the losses have been 24 percent of total assets. The central bank of Slovenia recently estimated that losses stood at 18.3 percent. In Spain and Portugal, the recognised losses are already more

than 10 percent, but the numbers will almost certainly be higher. Non-performing loans are also rising rapidly in Italy.

Germany is an interesting case. The German banking system appears healthy at first sight. It certainly fulfils its function of providing the private sector with credit at low interest rates. But I still find it hard to believe that the German banking system as a whole is solvent.[18]

Instead, Münchau wrote, regulators 'pretend not to see the losses, and extend the crisis'.

As a result, speculation by the private finance sector was once again unleashed and new asset bubbles created – these inflated the prices of stocks and shares, bonds, property, works of art, and the like. Post-2009 asset price inflation wildly enriched the rich while those without assets were further impoverished. Inequality predictably widened. When those reinflated asset bubbles burst, they too will cause further havoc.

These facts are widely known and understood, but not acted upon.

CHAPTER 5

Class Interests and the Moulding of Schools of Economic Thought

Economic fundamentals are all sound; it's a good time for tighter credit conditions ... the recent sell-off in financial markets is good news ... The world economy is strong enough to cope with the consequences.

The Economist, 4–10 August 2007

Editors and journalists at the *Economist* magazine were not the only professional economists to make entirely the wrong call in the week that inter-bank credit 'crunched' and the 2007–09 global financial crisis began in earnest.[1] Most academic economists shared their blind spot for the likely impact of financial deregulation on the financial system, the global economy and societies around the world.

A great deal of the power exercised by financiers operating in financial markets derives from the studied indifference of orthodox academic economists to the production of money and the social construct that is the rate of interest on money. Staggering though it might seem to a non-academic audience, the overwhelming majority of mainstream economists do not understand, nor do economists study, the nature of credit and money, or indeed the wider financial and monetary system. As the governor of the Bank of England at the time, Mervyn King, explained in 2012, 'The dominant school of modern monetary policy theory – the New Keynesian model as it is called – lacks an account of financial intermediation, so money, credit and banking play no meaningful role.'[2]

Yet policies based on this vacuum in economic theory still prevail in all western treasuries and in major university economics departments. Unbelievably, they are informed by the economist Paul Samuelson's barter-based theory of money and credit: 'Even in the most advanced industrial economies, if we strip exchange down to its barest essentials and peel off *the obscuring layer of money,* we find that trade between individuals or nations largely boils down to barter.'[3]

With money and money-creation helpfully obscured by economists, and regulation trained on meaningless capital adequacy targets, business is better than usual for credit-creating commercial bankers, even while their balance sheets effectively remain under water. Central banks continue to generate liquidity for speculation. Taxpayers continue to guarantee risk-taking by financiers and speculators. And in a strange reversal of the purpose of banking, bankers stopped lending during the crisis into, for example, the UK economy. Instead depositors and savers lent their surpluses to bankers, expecting very little in return. Despite all appearances, as Professor Joseph Vogl, a German historian, noted, 'the crisis proved itself as a way to solidify the existing economic order'.[4]

But while the economics profession remains largely unmoved, with honourable 'heterodox' exceptions in a few universities, and while the finance economy remains intact, the destructive impact of ongoing crises on societies all over the world has been immeasurable. According to the International Labour Organisation, around 200 million people were made unemployed in 2015. The Middle East and North Africa, at the vortex of political, religious and military upheaval, has the highest rate of youth unemployment in the world. Even before the economic crisis of 2007–09, there were 170 million people that had no work. Economic conditions in the world worsened dramatically as the financial crisis rolled on. Europe, with obstinately high levels of unemployment, faced frightening political tensions and divisions, and the rise of right-wing and even fascist parties. The mighty economy of the United States struggled to fully recover from the crisis, and was not immune to the rise of political populism and the threat of 'corporate fascism' – the merger of state and corporate power.

Yet economists (with some notable exceptions) stood aloof from these crises largely of their own making. And when they deigned to engage it was to adopt an attitude of defeatism. Often it was victims of financial deregulation – like the subprime borrowers of the US's Rust Belt – that were blamed for borrowing too much and causing the crisis. According to one of the most powerful mainstream and so-called 'Keynesian' economists Larry Summers, societies were living through 'The Age of Secular Stagnation' caused by a 'natural' rate of interest that was too low! The public were constantly enjoined to simply accept the fate of falling incomes, cuts in public investment, financial failure, bankruptcy and unemployment, for as the economists effectively argued: 'there is nothing to be done'.

But that was, and is, a lie. There was much that could have been done to alleviate the suffering of millions of people, especially young people, and to limit the destruction of value that occurred after the crisis. All that was necessary was to remove orthodox economic blinkers. Furthermore, we could look back to the precedent, and the experience of the 1930s, when Keynes and Roosevelt confronted, rather than capitulated to, financial elites. Roosevelt attacked the finance sector directly in his famous inaugural speech, which bears repetition:

A host of unemployed citizens face the grim problem of existence, and an equally great number toil with little return. Only a foolish optimist can deny the dark realities of the moment.

Yet our distress comes from no failure of substance. We are stricken by no plague of locusts ... Plenty is at our doorstep, but a generous use of it languishes in the very sight of the supply. Primarily this is because rulers of the exchange of mankind's goods have failed through their own stubbornness

THE PRODUCTION OF MONEY

and their own incompetence, have admitted their failure, and have abdicated. Practices of the unscrupulous money changers stand indicted in the court of public opinion, rejected by the hearts and minds of men.

... Faced by failure of credit they have proposed only the lending of more money. Stripped of the lure of profit by which to induce our people to follow their false leadership, they have resorted to exhortations, pleading tearfully for restored confidence. They know only the rules of a generation of self-seekers. They have no vision, and when there is no vision the people perish.

Both Roosevelt and Keynes set about resolving a debt-deflationary crisis eerily similar to the one we face today. In both countries they helped rebuild sustained economic recovery. Above all, they renewed confidence in the democratic process.

The revelations of the Bank of England

The Bank of England's two articles on the nature of money in their 2014 *Quarterly Bulletin*, 'Money Creation in the Modern Economy' and 'Money in the Modern Economy: An Introduction', were a revelation for many mainstream economists.[5] The Bank's economists confirmed that most of the money in the modern economy is created by private banks making loans. Moreover, the Bank emphasised that this was *'the reverse of the sequence typically described in textbooks'*. Let us be clear here: this was not a failure of some textbooks; it was a failure of virtually *all* economics textbooks.

As a result, economics students were and are still taught a fallacious theory of money. And this failure of teaching was and is symptomatic of an even greater failure: the failure of the academic economics profession itself, of its learned discussions, conferences, published papers and contributions to policy. And let us not beat about the bush: as the liberal John

Class Interests

Hobson (1858–1940), an English economist and social scientist, observed over a hundred years ago:

> The selection and rejection of ideas, hypotheses and formulae, the moulding of them into schools or tendencies of thought, and the propagation of them in the intellectual world, have been plainly directed by the pressure of *class interests*. In political economy, as we might well suspect, from its close bearing upon business and politics, we find the most incontestable example.[6]

The 'moulds of schools of thought' now dominant in both economics and wider society have led to vast capital gains for financial elites, and to a prolonged failure of the global economy and rising inequality. But thankfully, the triumph of class interests is not universal. The Bank of England rightly credits the handful of scholars that have railed against mainstream academia's understanding of money. Those few and brave economists argued their positions at great expense to their academic careers. They were not permitted to participate in learned discussions; their papers were not published in distinguished journals; nor were their views sought by government on policy. Professor Charles Goodhart describes how

> the suggestion that Prof. X took an institutional approach to monetary analysis was sufficient to cast his/her reputation into outer darkness. Only small groups of mainly heterodox (and of various hues of post-Keynesian views) economists have bothered much to relate theory to reality. Why this has been so, I do not know ... [it] is not a good advertisement for this sub-sector of our profession.[7]

To an impartial outsider or observer of the economics profession, this beggars belief. How can economists not bother 'to relate theory to reality'? How can economists analyse the economy without an understanding of money – the cornerstone and raison d'être of all economic activity? And how is it possible that those who *do* grasp these processes, are cast into 'outer darkness'?

Keynes and the sin of omission

While the Bank of England shone a light on this academic darkness, some distinguished economists were still obscured from view. The most glaring omission in the Bank's 2014 articles was any positive mention of John Maynard Keynes. A great part of his career was spent in debate over monetary theory and the proper conduct of monetary policy. His election to the Court of the Bank of England in 1941 was recognition of the remarkable contributions he had made in the course of those discussions.

His ideas evolved from a profound understanding of the nature of money. The opening chapters of his *Treatise on Money* (1930) were widely understood at the time as the fullest exposition of these matters, and subsequently commended as such by Josef Schumpeter.[8]

After the publication of the Bank of England 2014 *Quarterly Bulletin*, Mark Carney, governor of the Bank of England, defined the motive behind the establishment of the Bank of England in 1694 as raising money 'to carry on the war' with France.[9] Not so. While financing the war was important, the authorities at the time were more concerned with establishing a bank-money system like that already established by the prosperous Dutch, and along the lines of that described by the Bank of England staff today. Back in 1694 the goal of the Bank of England was to mimic Holland in reducing the rate of interest paid by Dutch commercial firms, and to bring English interest rates into line with those that prevailed in the financially more advanced Netherlands.

But this understanding of a system of bank money causing

rates of interest to fall was lost in the classical economics of one David Ricardo (a financier). As a result, the theories of credit and associated bank-money policies lived on only, as Keynes put it, in 'an underworld' of scholars and activists. These included Henry Thornton, Thomas Malthus and Henry Dunning McLeod, and the sociologists Peter Knapp and Georg Simmel, who were not content to leave the question of the nature of money to the economists.

Keynes's great achievement was to retrieve this understanding from its burial by economic scholars. He understood that basing a theory of the economy on a fallacious theory of bank money would lead to profound misjudgements in economic policy, and to financial and economic crises. The task he set himself in his *General Theory of Employment, Interest and Money* was to devise a theory of an economy based on a correct understanding of money.[10] In it, Keynes's conclusions about practical policy were vastly different from those of his contemporaries, and from their successors in today's economic establishment.

Keynes recognised that the monetary system should be steered away from serving particular vested or class interests, and be repositioned to serve the needs of society as a whole. This understanding led to policies for permanently low interest rates during the Second World War, near full employment after the war, a thriving private and public sector, financial stability in the post-war period, and the unprecedented narrowing of income distribution.

Predictably perhaps, his policies did not endure. And with his policies, went his theory and, once more, the understanding of money. Classical economics and its flawed theory of money was revived. The understanding of bank money and credit shared by those in the 'underworld' lived on only through Keynes's closest colleagues in Cambridge, who were subsequently cast out of the profession.

His theory was revived as post-Keynesian economics in

the US under Sidney Weintraub, Hyman Minsky and Paul Davidson, and in the UK by Victoria Chick, among others. Geoffrey Ingham in the UK has revived the tradition within sociology. This revival has been echoed by the accessible and popular account in the New Economics Foundation book *Where Does Money Come From?*[11]

Given the pressure of class interests that shape today's economic ideas, the long-standing neglect of his theory and policies, particularly at his alma mater Cambridge University, does not come as a surprise. The 'veil' that is today cast over the nature of money by orthodox economists means that Keynes's theoretical conclusions are lost. Classical economic theory and policies once again protect the same class and vested interests that were adversely affected by Keynes's policies. While the Bank of England's intellectual excavation, therefore, is welcome, it is not enough. The whole shaky intellectual superstructure on which the flawed classical theory is based should now be dismantled. A deeper understanding of Keynes's theory and policy conclusions will provide economists and society with tools for recreating an economy that can once again restore balance and stability; an economy that will serve the interests of society as a whole.

From the time of his rejection of the gold standard (in his 1923 book, *A Tract on Monetary Reform*), Keynes was concerned with the *prevention* of economic crises. In the wake of the Great Depression, he wanted to establish conditions for the restoration of prosperity and to prevent such events ever recurring again.

In this Keynes clearly failed. But this failure was through no fault of his own. For the Keynes that survived into conventional wisdom and most importantly, the Keynes that has survived into the lecture theatre, is a gravely distorted and diminished figure. He is now associated largely with fiscal actions to combat crisis, when to prevent crisis he was concerned primarily with monetary initiatives. His objectives were reform of the international financial architecture on the one hand, and the setting of low interest rates on the other. Managed finance and cheap money – on a permanent basis – were his central ambitions.

But either way, it is time the economics profession woke up to the extraordinarily high stakes of its intransigence and neglect of Keynes. The world desperately needs to recover Keynes.

Keynes's monetary theory

From a theoretical perspective, Keynes was a monetary economist, understanding that conventional or classical economics was irrelevant to an economy based on credit. His concern was to devise a theory for what he called a 'monetary production economy'.

In *The General Theory* he finally understood that the critical point of departure of any such theory from the classical theory was the long-term rate of interest: the rate that underpinned all private activity, especially investment.

Whatever the precise formulation, in the classical theory the rate of interest is *a passive consequence* of whatever real events are regarded as dictating outcomes. Today the most prominent of these events is defined as 'a global savings glut', changes in population growth, and failing productivity. In Keynes's theory it is the rate of interest that *dictates* events and that, unchecked, is the 'villain of the economic piece'. Unchecked, high rates of interest vindicate two millennia of condemnation of usury in both philosophical and religious doctrines.

Ultimately, Keynes understood the rate of interest as a social construct, set according to the balance of conflicting economic interests. Keynes did not use the language of class, but his theory meant that the class struggle was very much a reality. But his was changed from Marx's account in this respect: productive industry and labour shared interests, and these were opposed by finance – what Keynes called 'vested interest' or the rentier class. Low rates of interest or cheap money favoured industry and labour. Dear or costly money at high rates of interest favoured finance.

The progressive 'euthanasia of the rentier' was for Keynes the price society paid for securing full employment, decent public goods and services, and economic stability. Given that the rentier was hardly likely to engineer his or her own demise, then the assertion of public authority over the financial system was essential.

Until Keynes, finance had been jealously guarded by *private authority*. Today such public authority of the kind advocated by Keynes is rejected by mainstream economists, and even by many progressive economists who use the imprecise and pejorative notion of 'financial repression' to attack democratic management of the finance sector. Financial 'repression' is akin to regarding the emancipation of slaves as the repression of the rights of slave owners!

On a more mundane theoretical and practical level, the theory of liquidity preference led to the devising of appropriate monetary and debt management arrangements to enable any such authority to set the rate of interest across the spectrum of lending.

The ability of the public authorities to achieve low rates of interest across the spectrum is fact. As was Keynes's practical successes in reducing interest rates, both before and during the Second World War.

Economic orthodoxy, Keynes and the Great Depression

As of the 1919 Versailles conference after the First World War, financial interests dictated the economic terms for peace. With scarcely any recognisable difference from the gold standard, finance's 'economic terms' back then were made up of the usual orthodoxies familiar today. They included a requirement that central banks remain independent, that government spending should be restrained, that the mobility of capital be unfettered, and that high real rates of interest should prevail.

As soon as 1923, with Weimar hyperinflation, the economic arrangements collapsed with a rapidity and severity that is astonishing. Depression began first in Germany and then moved to include the United States after the Crash of 1929. Recovery and global monetary reform only began in the UK when membership of the gold standard was suspended on 21 September 1931. Over the next five years Keynes's ideas and policies led a major realignment of class relations in the US and Europe, aided by a profound political shift to the Left, including the election of Franklin Roosevelt as President in the US in 1933, and the election of Leon Blum as leader of the Popular Front in France in 1936.

The gold standard would be replaced by Keynes's scheme for currency management first devised for his 1923 *Tract on Monetary Reform*. Exchange rates were to be managed by central bank intervention in foreign exchange markets using massive funds provided by governments, rather than by manipulation of central bank discount rates. These interventions would be supported with a degree of capital control, and would therefore permit a major reduction in interest rates (short and long, safe and risky, and real rates) all over the world.

Following Britain's departure from the gold standard in 1931, the scheme for currency management in Britain operated through the Exchange Equalisation Account. The immediate priority was to achieve reductions of short and long term rates internationally, as individual economies so desperately required.

When in 1934 at the world economic conference Roosevelt famously torpedoed gold as the 'fetish of so-called international bankers', he was inviting the rest of the world – not least the gold bloc of European nations – to follow Britain's lead. This was a vital imperative to the writing of Keynes's *General Theory of Employment, Interest and Money*.

Keynes understood his theory as a framework for ensuring that market failure occurred only when it was improperly understood and wrongly operated. It is profoundly wrong to portray Keynes as an enemy of markets and freedom. His goal was 'not to defeat, but to implement the wisdom of Adam Smith'.

He confronted rival arguments (including within the UK) that alleged economic depression was due to the failure of laissez-faire, and that this failure necessitated a retreat to authoritarianism of various kinds, the most obvious being the rise of Adolph Hitler, who took power at almost exactly the same time as Roosevelt.

In the United States, France and the UK, democratic, public authority over finance was, de facto if not de jure, imposed by their respective central banks: the Federal Reserve, the Banque de France and the Bank of England. A decade later, one of the first acts of the British Labour government was to go all the way by nationalising the Bank of England. In Germany under Hitler, private authority over finance prevailed. Contrary to conventional wisdom, while Hitler may have initially been motivated to address the problem of unemployment, both he and his chancellor Hjalmar Schacht deliberately and explicitly turned their backs on monetary reform and stood firmly on the side of finance. By contrast, democratic governments had been freed from the restraints applied by financial orthodoxy, most triumphantly under President Roosevelt's New Deal.

By the time Keynes's *General Theory* was published in February 1936, the final disintegration of the gold standard had already begun. His remarks in March 1935, when Belgium came off gold, echo through history, 'Stupid and obstinate old gentlemen at the Banks of Netherlands and France crucifying their countries in a struggle which is certain to prove futile'.[12]

The 'cross of gold' was finally lifted when France adopted currency management upon the election of Blum in September

1936, at which point the gold standard collapsed. Under the Tripartite Agreement, the British and US governments had agreed to support the French exchange rate so that monetary reform was global and cooperative. Public authority over finance and cheap money prevailed over the greater part of the world.

The modern age

With the exception of the five years of the 1945 Labour government in Britain, the decisiveness of this re-alignment of class interests was ruptured in the post-war age. The most obvious statement of intent was the United States' rejection at the 1944 Bretton Woods Conference of the British Government's proposal for Keynes's International Clearing Union (ICA). The ICA was to be a global, independent bank that would hold all international reserves and would manage and 'clear' all debiting and crediting payments between countries, and by that means determine changes in exchange rates. Instead, to reflect the hegemonic role the United States played in a world ruined by war, the US dollar was given a central role in the post–World War II world. But even though the global trajectory was set to move away from Keynes and monetary reform, compromises towards expansionary fiscal policy, restraints on capital mobility, the management of trade imbalances, relatively low interest rates and an enhanced role for governments post-war led to great progress and prosperity.

The Golden Age (1947–71) was truly golden. Inflation and unemployment, 'both of which were later to explode with great force' in Britain, as David Smith notes, were low worldwide, including even Africa.[13] Economic activity, theatre, sport and music thrived. Inequality declined. Even the public finances were stabilised.

Sir Peter Middleton, permanent secretary to the Treasury from 1983 to 1991, described the mood there when he first joined in 1960:

It was a period of confidence and consensus in the Treasury. A post-war deflation had been avoided. The commitment in the wartime White Paper to employment policy to maintain a high and stable level of employment had been achieved to an extent greater than anyone expected – and was reiterated both in the 1956 White Paper on the economic implications of full employment and in the Radcliffe Report in 1959. We had lived within the Bretton Woods arrangements – a little precariously at times but successfully.[14]

But the achievement of full employment was disregarded by economists and policymakers then, much as it is disregarded today: as a non-event. They promoted instead an agenda based on 'growth' and financial liberalisation.

From the early 1960s with full unemployment at 2 percent, British policymakers echoed the OECD in setting an explicit target for real annual 'growth' of 4 percent. These unrealistic targets combined with financial deregulation inevitably led to the inflation of the 1960s and '70s. Inflation was a consequence of financial liberalization, policies far removed from those promoted by Keynes, but nevertheless blamed on him.[15]

Finance was freed from so-called 'repression' during the 1960s and low interest rates were replaced by high real rates across the world.

Keynes is still wrongly blamed for these policies. Although they are portrayed by economists as reflecting the failure of Keynes, they are in fact arguments deployed to justify the intensification of financial liberalisation and globalisation.

From the point of view of Keynes's theory, the most significant and dangerous change was the restoration of dear money in 1980. Since then, advanced economies have endured thirty-five years of generally high levels of unemployment, periodic financial crises and severe instability. This finally came to a head with the global financial crisis of 2007–09

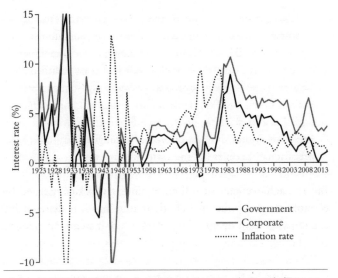

Source: Geoff Tily, 'The Long-Term Rate of Interest: Contrasting the Council of Economic Advisers and Keynes', Policy Research in Macroeconomics, 3 November 2015.

Fig. 5. The US real rate of interest from 1923 to 2013.

after the greatest expansion of private debts could no longer be sustained.

As in the 1930s, these debts were the result of easy and dear money.

Unsustainable debts build up when lending is not managed by public authority and loans cannot be repaid. Unpayable debts are more likely under dear, rather than cheap money.

The economics profession regards the subsequent failure of economic activity as the new norm – 'secular stagnation'. Interest rates are thought merely to reflect in a passive way this dismal outlook, one expected to extend indefinitely into the future. Governments have been and are still required to retrench, to manage low investment, unemployment and political instability within severe constraints and with greatly reduced means. And Keynes is associated merely with those who argue against taking fiscal consolidation too far.

Politicians do no more than to manufacture political capital – 'we're balancing the books', 'living within our means' – from the economists' insistence on contraction of economic activity during a slump via fiscal consolidation. Yet, of course, the retrenchment resolves nothing – in Europe, in Japan, or in the US. Private and public debts accumulate, and deflationary forces bear down on advanced economies.

In these contemporary contexts, emerging authoritarianism is rationalized by many as reflecting the weakness and ineptitude of western democracy in the wake of this terrible crisis. With the exception of campaigns like that of US Senator Bernie Sanders' bid for the US presidency in 2016, the immensity of the power of the finance sector – Wall Street the City of London – has not been contested to any material extent by either the wider Left, social democratic parties, or indeed even by the reactionary forces in society.

Keynes today

The power of Keynes's ideas is of a scale that has no precedent. The associated threat to vested, financial interests is obvious. To understand properly the *General Theory* is to recognise the genuine possibility of a profoundly better world – for this generation, but also for our grandchildren. The fact that the *General Theory* is not recognised – or even taught in Cambridge – tells us more about today's economists than about Keynes's stature as one of Britain's great geniuses on a par with Darwin. For as Austin Robinson wrote in the *Economic Journal* in 1972, 'If in the process of reappraisal Keynes does not emerge as a truly great man, something, let me repeat, will have gone sadly wrong with the criteria of greatness.'

CHAPTER 6

Should Society Strip Banks of the Power to Create Money?

The Sovereign Money movement

As this goes to press. the Great Financial Crisis is far from over. Its centre of gravity moved from Wall Street and the City of London in 2007–09, to the Eurozone in 2010, and then in 2015 to 'emerging markets' including China. The ongoing crisis has led to a rising tide of public fury, spread across continents, and mostly aimed at private bankers. But public anger is also increasingly directed at the political and technocratic establishments that actively protect the interests of financiers: politicians and technocrats that have tossed their 'free market' theory to one side and protected private financial risk takers from the discipline of the market and from the rule of law. There is outrage at the way private losses have been socialised and public funds and guarantees generously deployed to bail out private bankers and the financial system as a whole.

In Britain a 'Sovereign Money' movement of monetary reformers has grown out of discontent with the perpetrators of this grave crisis and has convened a remarkable anti-banking coalition under its banner. The coalition is made up of Marxists, left-wing and 'green' activists on the one hand; and on the other, anti-Keynesians, monetarist, orthodox academics and central bank officials. Their key demand is that a nation's money supply should be nationalised and that banks should be stripped of the power to create credit. Instead, this power should be transferred to a committee of technocrats at the central bank. After wider consultation, this committee would determine the economy's needs for finance – what Mary

Mellor, author of *Debt or Democracy* calls 'democratically determined provisioning'.[1] The committee would then create, and periodically adjust, the debt-free money supply required to meet the nation's needs for finance. Bankers would act as intermediaries between savers and lenders. The movement shows little concern for high interest rates; indeed they are seen as beneficial because they act as constraints on lending. They have also little interest in cross-border financial flows or the impact of these flows on domestic economic policies.

Sovereign Money reformers are backed by establishment figures such as Lord Adair Turner of the Institute of New Economic Thinking (INET) and Martin Wolf of the *Financial Times*. The latter argued that, 'proposals for replacing private debt-created money with government-created money are perfectly feasible and would bring substantial benefits.'[2]

Although I am about to take issue with their specific proposals, I am also clear that today's monetary reformers must be congratulated. They are taking aim at reckless and greedy bankers. They are generating public debate about a vital area of public policy. And they are excavating knowledge about money creation and the monetary system, knowledge that has long been buried in the field of 'agnotology': the study of ignorance-making, the study of the lost and forgotten.[3]

But money creation has, as earlier explained, long been understood. John Law, the Scottish genius, understood credit or bank money way back in the 1700s. While he is remembered (and vilified) for both a colourful private life and events that spun out of his control in France in 1720, he had a much better understanding of money than his much-celebrated fellow countryman Adam Smith. Law's books *Money and Trade: With a Proposal for Supplying the Nation with Money* (1705) and *Essay on a Land Bank* (1720) paved the way for the advanced monetary systems in place today.[4]

Presidents Thomas Jefferson (1743–1826) and Abraham Lincoln (1809–61) also understood the money system and had a healthy fear of Wall Street or what Lincoln called 'the money power'. But, like Keynes, Schumpeter, Minsky and Galbraith, they struggled to share their understanding of credit and money with their colleagues in the economics profession.

Given the extraordinary difficulty that many mainstream and orthodox economists face in recognising that bank loans create deposits, today's money-creation reformers are once again asking the right questions: Why is there public ignorance about money-creation and the monetary system? Who has manufactured this ignorance? And why do mainstream academic economists have a blind spot for credit, money, banks and debt? Above all, monetary reformers demand: Why has the banking system burdened society with vast amounts of oppressive debt, levels of debt that lead to recurrent 'financial and real crises'? These are profound questions that challenge the arrogance and incompetence of the economics profession, and the financial and political establishments responsible for ongoing crises.

While sympathising with much of the movement's concerns about out-of-control bankers and high, unsustainable levels of private debt, I find myself in strong disagreement with their proposals for addressing these issues. I fear they are turning the clock back and leading many into an intellectual dead-end. This will only increase public anger and frustration while simultaneously letting the perpetrators of financial crises – and their friends in the economics profession – off the hook.

Monetary reform campaigners advocate adoption of a particular variety of 'neoclassical economics' that proved backward-looking in the 1930s, and disastrous in the 1970s and 1980s. They are ideas that have long been discredited, even while still being promoted by leading economists today. So, if campaigners do lose their way through the thickets of economic policies and theory, the blame lies primarily (in my view) with the economics profession.

In this book I have tried to explain how a sound and just monetary system could operate, and serve the interests of society as a whole. In this chapter I will tackle and challenge specific issues raised by the monetary reform movement.

The campaign's aims

The key aim of money reformers is to strip private bankers of the power to create money and instead, as sociologist Mary Mellor writes, to choose 'public control of a debt-free money supply'. The crisis, argues Ms Mellor, 'reveals that the sovereign power of money creation has been harnessed in the service of the banking sector rather than the people. The time has come for the people to claim that sovereign right and replace debt by democracy.'[5]

The NGO Positive Money in its publication *Creating a Sovereign Monetary System* expands on the proposal:

> The central bank would be exclusively responsible for creating as much new money as was necessary to support non-inflationary growth. It would manage money creation directly, rather than using interest rates to influence borrowing behaviour and money creation by banks (as is the case at present). Decisions on money creation would be taken independently of government, by a newly formed Money Creation Committee (or by the existing Monetary Policy Commitee). The Committee would be accountable to the Treasury Select Committee, a cross-party committee of Members of Parliament who scrutinise the actions of the Bank of England and Treasury. *The Committee would no longer set interest rates, which would now be set in the market* [my emphasis].[6]

Mary Mellor, who agrees with Positive Money advocates:

> The simplest way to remove bank-created debt and its growth dynamic is to remove from the banking system the right to

create new public currency, or to severely limit it. Banks would be restricted to doing what most people think they do: lend savers' money to borrowers. Instead of money created through bank-issued debt, new public money could be issued by public monetary authorities, free of debt, directly into the economy to meet public needs.[7]

However, in contrast to Positive Money, Ms Mellor promotes a more 'participatory and deliberative democracy':

Exclusive control of public money must not be in the hands of the government in power, or the state apparatus. Neither public nor private finance are free of embezzlement and corruption. Creation of both public and commercial money needs to be transparent and accountable. Economic democracy must be much wider than the government in power ... Involvement of the public in decisions about the allocation of money would be a sea-change in what is meant by democracy.[8]

Regrettably, given the importance of their mission, the solutions offered by Sovereign Money reformers hark back to the outdated 'quantity theory of money' first developed by Jean Bodin in 1560, and elaborated by David Hume, John Stuart Mill and others. Joseph Huber, who writes in support of the monetary reform NGO Positive Money, explains on their website that:

The quantity theory of money, one of the oldest and most proven elements of economics, is as essential as ever. Accordingly, the key to sound money and stable finances is to gain control of the money supply ...

As regards sovereign money, its mission is full control of the money supply in order to achieve a growth-commensurate quantity of money in circulation, avoiding the cliffs of loose-money inflation/asset inflation on the Left as well as the shoals of tight-money deflation on the Right.[9]

'The Chicago Plan Revisited'

'Full control of the money supply' is a Herculean ambition, to be undertaken, it is argued, by a small group of technocrats at the top of the central bank, overseeing an economy where millions of transactions take place every day. This was also the grand ambition of the Chicago Plan, an incarnation of the quantity theory for 'sound money and stable finances' developed by Henry Simons and Irving Fisher in 1933. It was ignored by the US administration of the time, largely on the advice of John Maynard Keynes. In his 'Open Letter to President Roosevelt' in December 1933, he attacked the quantity theory:

> The other set of fallacies, of which I fear the influence, arises out of a crude economic doctrine commonly known as the Quantity Theory of Money. Rising output and rising incomes will suffer a set-back sooner or later if the quantity of money is rigidly fixed. Some people seem to infer from this that output and income can be raised by increasing the quantity of money. But this is like trying to get fat by buying a larger belt. In the United States to-day your belt is plenty big enough for your belly. It is a most misleading thing to stress the quantity of money, which is only a limiting factor, rather than the volume of expenditure, which is the operative factor.[10]

This, it seems, was merely a temporary setback as the Chicago Plan of 1933 has, remarkably, been revived. In 2012 it was dusted off the shelves by two economists at the IMF, Michael Kumhof (now at the Bank of England) and Jaromir Benes, and the debate about its ideas revived in a publication 'The Chicago Plan Revisited'.[11] Because Kumhof and Benes acknowledged that banks supply 'deposits … created through additional bank loans', Sovereign Money reformers greeted 'The Chicago Plan Revisited' with enthusiasm, as if it were a radical, new plan. Very soon Simons and Fisher's ideas were integrated into the British civil society campaign Positive Money, and adopted by a range of civil society activists, economics professors, journalists and think tanks.

The original Chicago Plan was written in righteous anger after the 1929 stock market crash and the Great Depression that followed. Simons and Fisher had direct experience of the easy money of the 1920s, and the role that reckless bank lending played in fuelling asset price inflation, stock market euphoria and mania. They proposed that private bankers be stripped of their power to create money. However their theory and Plan were built on shaky theoretical foundations.[12]

First, Simons and Fisher believed (and many still do) that money has no value in itself. It is merely a mechanism for arranging transactions, a 'veil' cast over the really important economic activity: the transactions between traders and entrepreneurs. They made a distinction between the money function (notes and coins issued by the government), the government's 'stock of reserves' which they define as 'money', and the (private) credit function. They seemed to assume that the last of these can be separated from the first two.[13] While recognising on the one hand that banks created 'their own funds' during credit booms, Simons and Fisher contradict this proposition by suggesting that *all money* is ultimately 'government-issued money'.[14] On this understanding the quantity of money is fixed by the central bank, resulting in a given quantity over any particular period of time. Changes in the quantity of money in the economy lead to other economic changes, in particular changes in national income in the form of higher prices.

Like earlier quantity theorists, Simons and Fisher struggled to understand or to fit *credit* into their theory of 'government-issued' money while recognising its existence. They were more comfortable with tangible money – government-printed notes and minted coins – and with the notion of money as government-issued 'reserves'. Money represented by bank

THE PRODUCTION OF MONEY

deposits created as a result of lending was treated as not having government 'reserve backing'. So Benes and Kumhof, in again taking up these ideas, are able to argue that under their new version of The Chicago Plan 'the quantity of money and the quantity of credit would become completely independent of each other.'[15]

Second, Simons and Fisher assumed that banks *single-handedly* created their own funds. In this view, there is no room for borrowers and their agency in the credit-creation process. There is no role for the investment or spending impulses of firms and consumers, or for broader economic policy-making that determines conditions for economic activity. There is no role for a nation of euphoric borrowers, or for reluctant, lacking-in-confidence borrowers. And there is no room for high rates of interest on safe or risky loans, or for productive or speculative activity, in precipitating crises. Finally, there is no role for the income and employment-creating activity generated by bank loans. Instead the assumption is that bankers alone are wholly responsible for the expansion of the money supply during booms, and that banks wilfully destroy these funds by contracting the money supply during downturns.

Third, despite denying the 'primitive commodity view of money' classical economists think of the supply of money as potentially scarce or excessive, just as there can be gluts and shortages of commodities.[16] Benes and Kumhof explain that bankers' behaviour can lead to an 'excess or shortage' of the money supply which in turn leads to either inflation or deflation. By focusing on the behavior of bankers, they ignore the regulatory context: the easy 'light-touch regulation' under which public authorities permit banks to lend. They ignore, too, the willingness or reluctance to borrow by firms or individuals, and their role in expanding or contracting the money supply. And nor do they discuss or analyse the wider economic conditions under which bankers lend.

This approach of focusing narrowly on the money supply ignores what money is lent *for*. Instead it is assumed that the supply and contraction of credit is simply a matter of wilful choice by bankers. By effectively nationalising the money supply, governments would be able, it is argued, to bypass the banking system to prevent shortages and increase supply.

We may note in passing that Simons' ideas were adopted by Milton Friedman and allied to his proposal for the strict management of fiscal policy in the event of a slump. Friedman advocated the adoption of 'fiscal rules' which, like Simons and Fisher's 100-percent reserve banking, are surprisingly fashionable once again. As David Smith explains in his book *The Rise and Fall of Monetarism,* Friedman's advocacy in a 1948 paper for a 100-percent reserve banking system was

> asking, in modern sophisticated economies for the clock to be turned back to the time when banks could only issue paper backed by an exactly equivalent amount of gold in their vaults. The second element was that (Friedman) ascribed an equal role in economic management to fiscal policy ... albeit a role that was based on strict rules rather than discretion.[17]

Friedman later argued that neither expenditure programmes nor tax structures should be varied in response to cyclical variations in economic activity.

Gluts and shortages of money

Simons and Fisher's theory of money prioritised its use in transactions, but were blind to a major insight that was provided by Keynes and revolutionised monetary theory: namely that money can also be used to satisfy the *speculative motive*. That kind of use was clearly very different from money held for the purpose of buying and selling. So while there may be a 'shortage' of bank loans (money) at affordable rates for purchasing solar panels, there may simultaneously be a 'glut' of money at high rates of interest for the purpose of speculation in, for example, London property. The debate about the money supply, inflation and the role of bankers would be very different if regulatory conditions barred lending for property speculation on the one hand and encouraged lending for the purchase of solar panels on the other – as Lord Adair Turner, of the Institute for New Economics, has argued.

As a result of this focus on money's origins as a means of buying goods and services, money as *a store of value* did not receive the same attention from the monetarists of the 1930s. Nor does it receive much attention from today's 'monetary reformers'. There was, and is, little discussion of what to do about borrowed bank money used for investment which then generates a surplus: capital. Capital can be held first, as cash; second, for security purposes and invested in safe assets; or third, as investment for speculative purposes. For most classical economists, and for their present-day followers, the management of capital and cross-border capital flows is a matter of third-order importance.

Positive Money campaigners are relaxed about 'offshore' capital and capital mobility, though of course they campaign against tax havens and tax evasion. Erratic and speculative capital flows across borders, while welcome to international financiers and creditors, strip domestic policy-makers of autonomy and the ability to adopt policies that best determine the interests and prosperity of the population of that country. These offshore flows lead of course to tax evasion, but also to harmful exchange rate volatility ('currency wars') that are especially dangerous for poor countries. Above all, capital mobility strips a country's public authorities of the power to manage economic prosperity by determining the most appropriate rates of interest (for productive lending across the spectrum of short-term and long-term loans, and taking into account inflation). That this key aspect of a financial system, considered fundamental by Keynes, is neglected by today's monetary reformers is regrettable.

The assumption that it is the supply of money that is important is repeated when Fisher and his modern-day supporters echo another misunderstanding at the heart of monetarist and Austrian economics (the orthodox economics of the Austrian School based on the rejection of macroeconomics). This is the assumption that aggregate economic activity tends to be stable, or moving towards an equilibrium in which supply matches demand and full employment follows. In this view, very little can be done by the authorities to change or improve levels of activity. Instead matters are left to the 'invisible hand' to move the economy to full employment.

According to this view, if the supply of money aimed at a given level of activity is too high, the result will be higher prices or inflation. The solution, monetarists argued, is to reduce the supply of money. However, aggregate economic activity (and especially employment) is never fixed or stable. It rises and falls, depending not just on the money supply but on wider economic conditions over which government and central bank regulation, fiscal and monetary policies have influence. Whereas Keynes aimed at trying to set regulatory, monetary and wider economic conditions to ensure optimum levels of employment and prosperity, his opponents, including Milton Friedman, preferred to leave aggregate economic activity and unemployment to the 'invisible hand' of the market. Instead they focused narrowly on the quantity of money, deemed to be government-issued. This emphasis and approach allowed monetarists in the 1980s to ignore and deregulate the activities of private bankers and instead focus on the public money supply, embodied in government spending. Benes and Kumhof remind us that as one of Mrs Thatcher's key advisers, the Chicago economist Milton Friedman in his later works took a diametrically opposed approach to that of Simons and Fisher: 'They advocated more governmental control over the money creation process via more control over bank lending. Friedman was interested in precisely the opposite, his concern was with making the government commit to fixed rules in order to otherwise keep it from interfering with (private) borrowing and lending relationships.'[18]

This Friedmanite bias for 'fixed rules' and associated monetarist policies were applied by Mrs Thatcher's government, and failed catastrophically to control inflation. Instead there was a dramatic rise in inflation, unemployment and bankruptcies.

Usurious rates

High, usurious rates of interest are regarded as of historical interest in 'The Chicago Plan Revisited', but appear to be of little importance or concern to their proposed arrangements. Kumhof and Benes argue that central bankers have 'only a single policy instrument, the nominal interest rate on short-term government bonds with which to affect both money and credit'.[19] While that need not be the case, by accepting they can do no more, both monetarists and today's central bankers rely on *only* the base or policy interest rate as a way of influencing economic activity. Kumhof and Benes propose that under their scheme, the government 'as the sole issuer of money can directly control the nominal interest rate on reserves ... and this rate [will] be passed on to depositors one for one'. Again, the bias towards a rate that suits depositors and savers, and not the many millions of borrowers that need to finance economic activities – some borrowers risky, others less so – is surely a careless blind spot.

Like orthodox economists, monetary reformers neglect the issue of interest rates for loans across the spectrum of lending. This at a time when central bank rates are exceedingly low (0.5 percent in the UK, 0.5 percent in the US, 0.0 percent in the Eurozone, 1.75 percent in Australia, 0.0 percent in Japan). By contrast, real rates are very high – allowing for deflationary pressures – on overdrafts and borrowing for firms, workers, entrepreneurs and students active in the real economies of these countries (22 percent for UK unsecured overdrafts, 4 percent for twenty-five-year mortgages. For corporates, the average spread over benchmark government yields for highly rated debt has widened to 1.84 percent – very high in real terms). These rates deter borrowing, thereby contracting the economy's level of investment and purchasing power. Those with no choice but to borrow at high rates include small and big firms, struggling students, and desperate would-be home-owners. In a deflationary environment, as incomes, earnings and cash flows fall in real terms, interest rates rise in real terms.

It is also disappointing that the 'radical' monetary reform movement shows so little interest in the role played by the rate of interest in the build-up of debt mountains. If the system is not managed, money lent at high rates of interest for largely speculative activity invariably results in burdens of unpayable debt, and in a vast overhang of private debt. This is especially so under conditions of 'austerity'. Monetary reformers are right to argue that such private debt overhangs are wrong; socially, politically, morally and economically wrong. Which is why high real rates of interest, even when central bank rates are low, should be denounced, and the system reformed and managed to keep interest rates across the spectrum of lending low.

Neglecting this important aspect of monetary theory and policy may be expected of classical and neoclassical economists who tend towards the interests of the wealthy, but it is disappointing in a civil society movement of monetary reformers seeking to fight a culture of recklessness and corruption.

Borrowers, not bankers determine the money supply

Under today's dominant economic model of 'liberal finance', banks can indeed produce credit and bank money out of thin air. However, no (licensed) bank can create credit unless there is a request or demand for a loan from a client. In other words, every time a banker or shadow banker engages in money-creation she is doing so in response to an application from one of her clients for that credit.

And there are hundreds if not thousands of such requests every working day at any one bank, for loans or overdrafts. In this sense money-creation is not a top-down process; it is the very opposite. All money is created (or not created) as a result of demand (or lack of demand) from below – from thousands if not millions of borrowers active in the economy. These borrowers have the power to influence the money supply.

Of course private bankers have the power to deny the borrower a loan, or to fix the interest rate and the terms on the loan at rates which make it uneconomic to borrow. Equally, under our deregulated system, they have the power to grant loans for reckless speculation.

Nevertheless, and even despite these great powers granted to private bankers, the monetary system is in a sense democratic. It is a bottom-up process, and to function requires 'two to tango'. The system depends for its health and profitability on the willingness or ability of individuals or firms to take the risk of borrowing money from a banker or creditor for the purpose of creating economic activity. If, as happened after the crisis of 2007–09, individuals or firms become reluctant to borrow, especially at high rates, *the supply of lending for economic activity falls*. The consequences are serious: a fall in investment and employment. As a result of fewer applications for loans or money, bankers and their borrowers exert a *deflationary* impact on the economy.

And if, during a boom, the demand for loans expands beyond the capacity of the economy – in other words, clients apply for and bankers create too much credit, which is then used to chase too few goods, services and speculative assets – *the money supply expands*. In this case, excessive borrowing and credit creation is likely to have an *inflationary* impact. If money is lent or borrowed at high real rates of interest, then it does indeed quickly become unpayable debt.

And as monetary reformers correctly argue: borrowed funds, if not properly regulated, can be and continue to be used for reckless speculation – the kind of speculation that ultimately causes global financial crises. (Little has been done since the Great Financial Crisis to limit such reckless lending. Indeed, global private sector debt has expanded massively since then.) Given the interconnectedness of the global financial system, crises can inflict massive damage, losses and anguish on both debtors and creditors worldwide, but also on many innocents in the wider economy and society.

Since money creation can be and is used for reckless and sometimes catastrophic speculation – is it right to argue for the abolition of all private money creation? For decisions on the money supply to be taken centrally and for banks to be constrained in lending, and for firms and individuals to be restrained in borrowing? No, would be my answer, and for this reason: 'involvement of the public in decisions about the allocation of money', to quote Mary Mellor, is what happens when individuals apply to banks for loans, which, if granted, play a role in increasing the money supply. To remove this public involvement at a micro level in the creation of a nation's money supply, and to instead rest this power with a small committee of men at the pinnacle of a central bank would to my mind be steps on to the road to an autocracy.

Furthermore, centralising the control of the money supply with only 'the inflation target' as a constraint would place great financial and economic power in the hands of a few technocrats, most of whom are steeped in orthodox economic dogma. As a result of this dogma, it is these technocrats who all failed in their roles as 'guardians of the nation's finances' before and during the crisis of 2007–09. Almost all of today's central banking technocrats have demonstrated an inadequate response to the crisis. They have failed to re-structure, to adequately re-regulate and therefore stabilise the global financial system, and have, on their own admission, exacerbated rising global inequality. This has in turn led to the rise of populism and extremism – all of which pose very real, grave threats to economies and societies. Further empowering these unaccountable officials, many of whom are used to undertaking monetary operations in secretive, opaque conditions, can only further diminish the accountability of elected lawmakers and exacerbate the democratic deficit.

Instead, it would be far better for a democratic government and its central bank to end the despotic power that bankers have derived from deregulation and from the convenient way in which economists have turned a blind eye to their activities. Rather, they should strengthen the power of those active in the real economy: in other words, to strengthen the hand of 'the makers' in relation to the private banking system, that is, the entrepreneurs and workers that create employment, provide services and undertake risky innovation.

A democratic government would make clear that the power of bankers and capital markets is almost entirely derived from the public goods and services provided by governments and their central banks. And because the creation of money is an activity entirely different from any other economic activity or business, democratic governments and their civil servants must, as 'guardians of the nation's finances', then manage and regulate the taxpayer-backed private banking system in the interests of society as a whole. The purpose must be to ensure that lending is managed to largely preclude speculation, and that decisions about the availability of finance and the setting of interest rates are regulated in such a way as to not discriminate against 'the makers' but instead to serve the interests of society, the economy and the ecosystem as a whole.

Private deficits cannot finance economic activity

The system of fractional reserve banking so enamoured of monetary reformers, implies that bankers would only be allowed to lend the savings or deposits lodged in their vaults by savers or depositors. We know from recent experience that the private sector can move into deficit: that the private sector's expenditure can exceed income, leading to a fall in savings. Back in 2003, Professor Wynne Godley explained how the financial balance of the US private sector moved from 'its historically normal range of about 3 to 4 percent of GDP, to a wholly unprecedented *minus* 5.5 percent of GDP in the third quarter of 2000 ... and in the fourth quarter of 2002 was still *minus* 1.1 percent, implying that private expenditure at that point was still higher than private income.'[20] In these circumstances and under proposed Sovereign Monetary reforms, negative savings rates imply that lending will have to contract to the same negative rates as savings. Some reformers propose that banks can then simply raise rates to attract funds from savers. This no doubt implies that rates on new loans would have to be higher to compensate for the higher cost of funding. Alternatively, the proposed Money Creation Committee can 'agree to create new money and lend it to banks with the requirement that this money would be on-lent to businesses that contributed to GDP (but not for mortgages or financial speculation).'[21] However, the principle of full-reserve banking would prevail on the whole with very little certainty as to whether the members of the Money Creation Committee would be willing to 'create new money' for the banking system. The Independent Commission on Banking argued that this would undoubtedly increase rates of interest on loans, but would also curtail the lending capacity of the UK banking system. It would result in unprecedented contraction of economic activity – employment, investment and spending – to levels of existing, and invariably scarce, *savings* (and in some nations savings are even more limited).

This was the approach adopted during the era of the gold standard which led to the Great Depression: economic activity, employment and government spending was cut back to correspond to the value of a limited and sometimes shrinking quantity of gold bars lodged in the central bank. Under the proposed Sovereign Money system, money or finance would once again be scarce. Scarcity would raise interest rates on existing savings to record levels, as Positive Money advocates Andrew Jackson and Ben Dyson argue in their book *Modernising Money*. It would also empower and enrich those fortunate enough to have accumulated savings. Rising unemployment, depression and economic failure would act to further limit the amount of savings in the economy.

These cannot be described as radical, progressive theories or policies.

In a democracy the arrangements under which money is issued are incredibly important to prosperity and to social and economic justice. And yes, it is correct to say that too much credit aimed at, for example, speculation in London's property market can be inflationary, and too little credit can be deflationary. Yet this is not down to the total *quantity* of the money supply but rather to the conditions under which loan financing is agreed. Rather, it would be down to *the quality* of money-lending: to the terms and conditions, and to the arrangements enforced by the 'guardians of the nation's finances' under which the monetary system is made to work to provide prosperity for all who are active within the economy – not just the few with savings.

Should or can money be debt free?

While debt can indeed become burdensome and exploitative of the borrower, it is also a vital source of finance for the economy – which is why its creation by the private sector must be carefully and rigorously managed by a democratic nation's public authorities. Monetary reformers, however, treat all debt as bad and make a big pitch for 'a debt-free money supply', to quote Mary Mellor. But debt-free money is an oxymoron. There is no such thing as debt-free money, or if there is, it is very likely something quite different – a grant or a gift.

Now there is no real reason why society should not aspire to building a gift-based economy – one in which all the individuals in that economy rely on others for 'provisioning' – for clean air and a safe environment, for the gifts of food, health, housing, for works of art, for a steam engine, or for a smartphone. But to date, while we still enjoy the remnants of a gift-bearing culture, we have failed to develop an entirely gift-based economy. The closest we have come to such economies are ones in which we collectively gift joint resources to each other via, for example, free education, a free Health Service, subsidised housing and so on. Such a society is defined as socialist or social democratic. But even in a socialist economy, socialised 'gifts' are ultimately a claim on us all – claims settled via the taxation system.

In a monetary system, as explained in an earlier chapter, all money is based on a system of claims: assets and liabilities backed up by collateral, and on the exchange of these in social relationships that are vital to the economic sustainability of households and communities. All money is a claim on another – an obligation to be reciprocated – or a debt. And debt, not barter, has been a feature of community life since the dawn of time, as David Graeber explained in his book *Debt: The First 5,000 Years*.[22] Adam Smith saw 'the origins of language – hence of human thought – as lying in our propensity to "exchange one thing for another" in which he also saw the origins of the market. The urge to trade, to compare values, is the very thing that makes us intelligent beings, and different from other animals', writes Graeber.[23]

The issue, therefore, is not the creation of a debt-free economy, but of one in which economic and other obligations can be freely and easily reciprocated to achieve the common purpose of stability, sustainability, justice and prosperity. This can only be achieved if the obligations and reciprocity of the monetary system are not exploitative; if the power between creditors (bankers) and debtors – both vital to the economy – is balanced. It cannot be achieved if the financial system is left to the decisions of a small number of technocrats, to the vested interests of private bankers, to the anarchic forces of the market, or to the despotic power of the few who operate in global financial markets. And social justice and prosperity cannot be achieved if the monetary system only provides access to finance for the already rich, those who own assets. The creation of a socially just monetary system – one that promotes widespread prosperity by acting as servant, not master of society and the economy; a monetary system that enables us all – including the public sector – to do what we can do, and be what we can be. *That* should be the aim of any progressive movement.

Does money just circulate?

It is wrong to suggest, as some monetary reformers do, that money is created by being borrowed into existence, *circulated* through the economy and then returned (in full) with interest, to the bank that created it? Borrowed money does not just 'circulate'. It creates purchasing power that gets *used up as investment and in the creation of employment, economic activity and income*. Above all, it provides purchasing power that can, if well used, generate *additional income*.

Bank money can also, for example, finance cures for plagues and diseases, as it has in poor countries such as Sierra Leone and Liberia. In doing so, money does not just 'circulate'. Instead it helps achieve things of immeasurable value: healthy communities and ultimately a healthy society. Money can help create employment. In doing so, it does not just 'circulate'. It helps create activity – artistic, scientific, practical or therapeutic.

The bitcoin mania

Bitcoins have introduced millions of people to a currency that appeared from nowhere and is, apparently, 'cryptographic proof'. Whereas private banks can create money by a stroke of the keyboard, the creation of bitcoins involves vast amounts of computer processing power. This power is capable of deploying a complicated algorithm that approximates the effort of 'mining' coins.[24]

The bitcoins so mined have become the new gold and bitcoiners the new goldbugs.

This new currency (which claims to be a commodity) is a form of peer-to-peer exchange. Its life began in the murky world of Silk Road, an online black market on the deep web, and has generated a great deal of excitement. It was created by an unknown computer scientist – the first bitcoin miner. It is now used for international payments, but also for speculative purposes. Like other virtual currencies, bitcoin has theoretical roots in the Austrian school of economics. Its advocates are keen followers of Friedrich von Hayek, and cite as inspiration his book, *Denationalisation of Money*, in which he calls for the production, distribution and management of money to be left to the 'invisible hand', so as to end the oversight of regulatory democracy.[25]

There are two things striking about this new currency. First, its creators (who are computer programmers) have apparently ensured that there can never be more than 21 million coins in existence. (Although bitcoins can be divided into smaller units: the millibitcoin, microbitcoin and satoshi. Satoshi is the smallest amount, representing 0.00000001 bitcoin, one hundred millionth of a bitcoin.)

Bitcoin is therefore like gold: its value lies in its scarcity. The potential shortage of bitcoins has added to the currency's speculative allure, leading to a general rise in its value. However, the volatile rises and subsequent falls in its value have made it unreliable as a means of exchange. It is tricky for traders to have to regularly adjust prices upwards or downwards when trading goods and services.

Second, this money or currency is not buttressed by any of the institutions named above. Its great attraction to users is precisely that it bypasses all regulatory institutions. Indeed, its usage appears to be based on distrust. One commentator notes that 'bitcoin was conceived as a currency that did not require any trust between its users'.[26]

Equally, its scarcity means that, unlike the endless and myriad social and economic relationships created by credit, the capacity of bitcoin to generate economic activity is limited (to 21 million coins). The currency's architects deliberately limited the amount of bitcoins in order ostensibly to prevent inflation. In reality, the purpose is to ratchet up the value of bitcoins, most of which are owned by originators of the scheme.

In this sense, bitcoin miners are no different from goldbugs talking up the value of of a finite quantity of gold, from tulip growers talking up the price of rare tulips in the seventeenth century, or from Bernard Madoff talking up his fraudulent Ponzi scheme.

However, some have hyped up the technology used by bitcoin – blockchain, a distributed database or ledger – and argued that it could revolutionise the distribution of wealth and provide transparent accounts of transactions. We should treat these claims cautiously. In a recent blog, *Financial Times* journalist Izabella Kaminska argued that financial technology fads follow a pattern similar to new music designated first as 'hip' and 'cool' but which then fades and becomes 'so last year'. In the same way, for her as an investigative journalist,

> Blur (bitcoin) evolved into a love of Radiohead (blockchain). But Radiohead (blockchain) was adopted too quickly by those who then compromised the likeability of the entire Indy genre (cryptocurrency).

It was time consequently to turn to drum and bass (private blockchains). But drum and bass was being cross-polluted by Indy rock enthusiasts (cryptocurrency enthusiasts) so it became time to embrace something totally radical and segregated, i.e. go backwards to an ironic appreciation of Barry Manilow abandoning all refs to modern musical phenomena (Distributed Ledger Technology).

Which puts us roughly at the point where cheesy revivalism should be turning into a general love of the all time provable greats (old school centralised ledger technology, but you know, digitally remastered).

Suffice to say, there is some commentary emerging to suggest we are indeed in a phase transition and what's cool isn't the blockchain anymore but rather the defiant acknowledgement that the old operating system – for all its flaws – is built on the right regulatory, legal and trusted foundations after all and just needs some basic tweaking.[27]

In 2016, $70 million worth of bitcoin was stolen from customer accounts held at Bitfinex. As Kaminska writes, that 'should give the banking industry pause for thought with respect to adopting blockchain and bicoin-based financial technologies'.[28]

Speculators have periodically inflated the value of bitcoin to delirious heights. As always, the winners are those who sell just before the bubble bursts. In the absence of democratic oversight and regulation, the losers are always robbed.

Credit, consumption and the ecosystem

Environmentalists rightly want to restrict forms of economic activity, in particular apparently limitless consumption – and I agree wholeheartedly with that aim. Indeed, it is my view that it is 'easy money' that fuels 'easy' shopping; 'Easy Jet' and with it toxic emissions. So management of the credit-creation system is vital to society's attempts to limit consumption and toxic emissions. Environmentalists who try to limit consumption by ignoring the links between consumption and easy money are doomed to failure, in my view.

Since the liberalisation of finance in the 1960s and '70s, bankers have aimed credit largely at pre-existing assets (such as land and property) and at consumption on which they can charge high rates of interest (think of the rate on your credit card). It is critical to note that both the US and UK economies are now largely based on household consumption. Before credit cards became universally available, and before political and central banking authorities freed up bankers to provide credit for any type of shopping expedition, consumption was constrained. So yes, society must limit its obsession with easy money, ubiquitous credit (or, rather, 'debt') cards and excessive and unnecessary consumption. And bankers must be constrained in their ability to lend money at high rates for activity that does not generate income for the borrower – i.e. consumption – or for other income-draining activities, such as nose jobs and other cosmetic surgeries for which there is no medical necessity.[29]

At the same time, human-induced climate change represents a major threat to a liveable future. Transforming the economy away from fossil fuels will require wisdom, intelligence and muscle. Above all, it will require a great deal of finance, for example to transform the transport system, erect flood defences, retrofit ageing housing stock, or to make buildings more energy efficient. Such investment will, however, generate employment and other economic activity. Employment in turn will generate income with which to repay the credit or debt. The fact is that carefully managed and regulated public and private credit will help finance vital de-carbonising activities. The small, individual pools of money from savings accounts, credit unions or crowdfunding would be woefully insufficient for the Herculean task of transforming the economy away from fossil fuels.

The 'People's QE' and 'helicopter money'

With the discovery that private banks can create money ex nihilo – out of thin air – came a simultaneous discovery: that central banks can do the same. Quantitative easing was treated as an extraordinary and novel development when the Federal Reserve announced in November 2008 that it was to embark on a programme of asset purchases from the banks for which it would exchange reserves and pump liquidity into the banking system. As explained earlier, central bank 'reserves' are not savings but more akin to 'overdrafts' for banks alone, and should not be confused with, for example, Saudi oil 'reserves'. Contrary to monetarist theory, central bank reserves are only used by banks, mainly for clearing purposes, and cannot leave the banking system to be channelled into the real economy.

When the Fed offered to buy a large number of securities held by banks, both mortgage-backed securities and government bonds, bankers exchanged these bonds – some of which were likely to be non-performing and therefore loss-making – for the equivalent of a bigger 'overdraft'. This ought to have cleared up bankers' balance sheets, and encouraged them to lend more into the real economy. But QE did not have that effect. In the UK bank lending actually fell. Instead the Fed and Bank of England (BoE) effectively provided the private finance sector with additional purchasing power with which financiers could go shopping for speculative assets in the FIRE sector: finance, insurance, and real estate. Lending into a weakened real economy, weakened further by austerity, was regarded by financiers as far less profitable and far more risky.

QE, it must be emphasized, is not a remarkable or unusual undertaking for central banks, although the *scale* of their monetary operations since the Great Financial Crisis *is* unprecedented. QE is just another variation on a central bank's routine and regular 'open market operations' (OMOs) when government securities (bonds) are bought and sold from banks and other affiliated financial institutions in the open market. Although there is uncertainty about the Bank of England's earliest open market operation, it is known that they have been undertaken for nearly two hundred years. Some historians believe the first OMOs took place in the 1830s to make the bank rate effective. Others have suggested to me that OMOs have taken place since the Bank of England was founded in 1694. Yet others are not so sure.[30] The Fed came late to OMOs, according to the Minneapolis Fed:

> Open market operations, the principal tool of US monetary policy, was discovered accidentally (in 1922) and was the biggest development in terms of the Fed's evolution from a passive to an active institution ... Fed officials realized that by purchasing securities on the open market, Federal Reserve Banks could affect general credit conditions across the country. In other words, when the Fed bought securities it increased commercial bank reserves and eased credit; the opposite applied when the Fed sold securities.[31]

However, what is unquestionable is that the scale of current open market operations is historically unprecedented. Between 2008 and 2015, the US Fed bought government bonds and mortgage-backed securities worth more than $4.5 trillion from the private finance sector. Between March and November 2009, the Bank of England's Monetary Policy Committee embarked on the purchase of £375 billion of financial assets from the banking sector – mostly UK government debt or 'gilts'.

As post-crisis public anger rose, and as activists came to understand that central banks had effectively used their power to bail out, finance, guarantee and enrich the private finance sector's activities but not the rest of the economy, which in contrast was being squeezed, demands grew for

QE to be used for wider public benefit. The call was for 'the People's QE', 'Sovereign Money Creation', 'Overt Monetary Financing', 'Helicopter Drops' and 'Green QE'. Again, the motive behind this activism is justifiable and the aim is indeed honourable – to ensure that a publicly resourced central bank benefits the whole of society and not just bankers.

But let us examine the proposals for 'helicopter money' more carefully.

Just as with calls for the nationalisation of the money supply, the calls for central bankers to use their powers for wider purposes come from across the political spectrum. Positive Money's economist Frank van Lerven has produced a helpful list of the main protagonists and an excellent overview of the public money creation debate.[32]

- *Strategic QE* – Proposed by the New Economics Foundation
- *Green QE* – Proposed by Victor Anderson, endorsed by Molly Scott Cato (MEP)
- *Helicopter Drop* – Proposed by Ben Bernanke (and a number of others) and based on Milton Friedman's 'Helicopter Drops' paper of 1948.
- *People's QE* (based on Green Infrastructure QE) – Proposed by Richard Murphy and Colin Hines.
- *Overt Monetary Financing* and *Sovereign Money Creation* – Proposed by Adair Turner and Positive Money respectively, and sufficiently similar to be treated as one proposal.

As van Lerven notes, 'These unconventional monetary policy proposals are similar in that they all advocate the proactive creation of central bank money to stimulate growth in the real economy.'

Strategic QE 'proposes that the Bank of England (via the Asset Purchase Facility) creates money and uses it to buy bonds from publicly owned intermediaries, such as a

Public Investment Bank, Green Investment Bank, or Housing Investment Bank'.[33]

Green QE 'proposes that the ECB and other national central banks within the EU use their money creating powers *to finance lending to the private sector* for green infrastructure projects and green businesses'.[34]

Ben Bernanke's *Helicopter Drops* takes

> inspiration from Milton Friedman's (1948) 'Helicopter Drop' thought experiment (considering what might happen if newly printed cash were to be dropped out of a helicopter in order to boost spending in the economy). Helicopter Drops would be used to finance a cash transfer from the government to each citizen (or each adult), via a 'citizen's dividend' (a non-repayable grant to every citizen), so long as the payment infrastructure exists to make a payment to every citizen. As an alternative, in Bernanke's original proposal, the government cuts taxes, leaving members of the public with higher disposable income and therefore greater spending power. The newly created money is given to the government to compensate for the drop in tax revenue. A money-financed helicopter drop would require collaboration between the Treasury and the Bank of England. In keeping with its current operational independence, the process would begin *with the BoE determining the size and timing of the helicopter drops.*[35]

The *People's QE* proposal is a

> type of programme in which the Bank of England would '... inject money into the UK economy that can kick-start economic activity in this country, reinvigorating government, local government, the private sector and household economies ...' To this end central bank money would be used to finance investment spending and lending. Primarily, central bank money would be used to finance the purchase of bonds issued

by public sector institutions to directly finance government spending on infrastructure projects, or new money would be created to finance the lending of a green or public investment bank (as in Strategic QE and Green QE).[36]

Adair Turner's *Overt Monetary Financing* (OMF) and Positive Money's *Sovereign Money Creation* (SMC) both offer the option of distributing the newly created money directly to citizens, or using newly created central bank money to finance public investment spending.

The 'People's QE' proposals weaken democratic authority
Public money creation activists have managed to mobilise impressive public and professional support for their proposals. The issues are discussed sympathetically at the highest levels of policy-making. On the way they have enlightened very many people, including myself, and spread understanding of complex financial processes. Very few have challenged these ideas on financial or economic grounds, although there is some concern about abuse of the 'money printing' process. My concerns are more broad-based, and largely economic and political. It takes some audacity on my part to disagree with many in this community who are respected friends and colleagues, so, with some trepidation, I beg their forbearance in advance.

My first concern is this: once again these proposals place great store on technocratic decision-making and power. Technocrats in central banks do not periodically stand for election. They tend to be faceless bureaucrats or academics never fully called to account for their theories or actions. Elected governments and finance ministers are similarly misguided and flawed, but many were held to account and paid a price, and indeed politicians are still (in 2016) paying a price as they face the threat of being displaced by right-wing populists.

Yet four out of these six 'public money creation' proposals will fuel disillusionment with democratic government further by simply bypassing elected representatives. This is the case for Strategic QE, Green QE, Overt Monetary Financing and Sovereign Money Creation proposals. By contrast, the People's QE and Bernanke's Helicopter Drops directly involve government at different levels. For Adair Turner's OMF and Positive Money's SMC, the aim is for the central bank to distribute money directly to citizens, but there is also an option to finance government spending.

However, all six leave decisions about *the quantity of 'money'* to be created to technocrats at central banks. In other words, while governments may provide the backbone to public money, and be beneficiaries of the 'People's QE', they are not in the driving seat. Central bankers are. These proposals place great power in the hands of these technocrats when, to my mind, elected representatives should be masters of this process with the central bank as servant – albeit an independent, open-minded and well-qualified servant.

Donald Trump and 'helicopter money': the economic, social and political consequences

It is also not acceptable, in my view, for central bankers or government representatives to be granted money-printing powers without clear, transparent checks and balances. Like the power private bankers exercise, central bank 'helicopter drop' powers are immense. They will have distributive consequences, and these will be difficult to predict. There are other consequences. Providing funds directly to citizens could for example, encourage them to shop for goods from abroad, worsening trade deficits. Other imbalances could occur.

These are impacts that have economic as well as social and political consequences. Therefore, given that we are discussing a publicly backed institution (the central bank, nationalised in the case of the UK), elected governments ought to be in the driving seat. At the same time, for public accountability reasons, the relative independence of the central bank must be maintained.

The reason for relative independence, accountability and transparency is not complicated: helicopter drops are very likely to be open to abuse. As someone who has worked in African countries where politicians are known to have corruptly diverted public resources, I consider transparent checks and balances on politicians, government officials and central bankers to be vital.

Lord Adair Turner, in a *Project Syndicate* column 'Helicopters on a Leash', drew attention to this central issue: the risk that allowing any monetary finance will invite excessive use.[37] But in addressing the issue, Turner cedes even more power to central bankers by proposing that they are 'given the authority to approve a maximum quantity of monetary finance if they believe doing so is necessary to achieve their clearly defined inflation target'.[38] There are two problems with this attempt at regulating the creation of finance: the first is the one outlined above, that technocrats will make critical decisions about the scale of finance available to all or some sectors of the economy. Second, the notion that 'inflation targeting' would once again be used to inform central bank decision-making is a truly backward step. Inflation targeting has long been discredited because pre-crisis central bankers focused myopically on inflation targets to the detriment of other indicators, in particular employment, but to the advantage of creditors whose assets (debt) are protected by inflation targeting.

I am no defender of the private finance sector, as anyone familiar with my work will know, and I am also strongly in favour of capital control. But under the far-from-perfect existing monetary system, domestic bond markets act effectively as intermediaries between a government and its central bank. The process of a government offering bonds to the public and private markets bidding for those bonds, places transparent space and publicly accountable transactions between a government and its central bank. It is the bond market that keeps governments honest. Of course investors can and do profit from this process and cream off gains, but losses are also possible. And as QE has proved, central banks working with willing governments can exercise huge influence over the bond market, and over the price and yields of government bonds. The fact that over the recent past global bond markets have played the role of 'master' in relation to subservient governments and central bankers is because both governments and central bankers have abrogated their power to restrain capital mobility and to manage this market. They have been negligent of the wider public interest, and left management of bond markets and the monetary system to a process described as 'globalisation' and to the anarchic 'invisible hand'.

But we know that bond markets can be subdued, and can play a more passive role than they have in the recent past. Just how subdued was evidenced in 2015 and 2016 when investors *paid* the German government for the privilege of lending it money – largely because of weaker, and riskier economic conditions in Europe brought on by incompetent economic policy-making and ideologically driven political decision-making. The monetary operations of the European Central Bank (ECB) also played a role. Investors were willing to pay to lend to Germany because economic conditions and returns on capital in Europe, and indeed the world, were so insecure, they believed capital would be more secure invested in a German 'bund'.

The problem is not the belt of QE, but the emaciated economy

But the most important *economic* difference I have with many respected friends in the public money creation movement takes us back to Keynes's powerful analogy: 'This is like trying to get fat by buying a larger belt. In the United States today your belt is plenty big enough for your belly. It is a most misleading thing to stress *the quantity of money, which is only a limiting factor*, rather than *the volume of expenditure, which is the operative factor*.'[39]

Lord Turner asserts that Overt Monetary Financing 'is the one policy that will always stimulate nominal demand, even when other policies – such as debt-financed fiscal deficits or negative interest rates – are ineffective.'[40] He puts the cart before the horse, or the larger 'belt' (publicly created money) before a skinny, emaciated, demand-weak global economy.

At the time of writing, the global economy is once again at risk of slipping into recession. There are intense deflationary pressures across the world, in part as a result of the contraction of bank lending into the real economy; weak demand for goods and services, and the growth of gluts of goods (and even services). Weak demand can in part be attributed to the ongoing financial crisis. Demand can be defined as the total amount of finance, labour, goods and services desired by consumers and producers at a given price level, and over a given time period. Financial instability renders the already over-indebted private enterprise sector timid and nervous, reluctant to take risks. To compound matters, the heavily indebted and fearful private banking sector prefers speculation and its potential for quick capital gains to sound investment in employment and economic activity. Bankers need a thriving economic environment, one in which there are borrowers with good collateral and potential income willing to borrow, confident of their ability to invest, to generate profits and income with which to repay the bank at the rate of interest charged. Instead politicians and policy-makers, in obeisance to Milton Friedman's regressive 'fiscal rules' driven by an ideological commitment to 'sound money and stable finances' have induced economic austerity. Cuts in public spending so that societies can 'live within their means' and 'balance the books' have in fact achieved the very opposite. Economic contraction because of cuts in public investment, spending and employment has instead lowered incomes and tax revenues, worsened government debt and increased deficits. In Britain, the Chancellor complained in his 2016 Budget that the 'the economy is smaller than we thought'.[41] He seemed unaware that it was his austerity policies that had made the economy 'smaller'.

The consequences of weak demand can be illustrated by one particular case: that of the mountains of rubber tyres in China in 2015. These were less needed than before because of weak demand, especially from European and American users of rubber tyres. Weak demand and a glut in rubber tyres led to falls in the price of rubber as well as in the price of tyres. Falling prices and profits in the rubber and tyre industries invariably led to unemployment in those industries. Rising unemployment led to lower wages and incomes, and this in turn weakened demand for a nation's goods and services. As a result, prices fell further, leading to more bankruptcies and unemployment ... and the downward cycle became almost unstoppable.

Expanding the public money creation 'belt' in a period of economic emaciation such as that described above will not kick-start investment and employment, or generate new income. Indeed, the world already has too much money – in the form of debt – as monetary reform activists repeatedly remind us. One reason private banks are not lending into the economy is that potential clients are already too heavily indebted. Another is that potential clients are refusing to borrow because they, while heavily indebted, are fearful of economic conditions because few customers are 'coming through the door'.

What is needed is for economic agents to begin spending on the employment of labour, and on goods and services (perhaps more on services than on goods, given climate change). The object must be to produce more employed people on sustainable incomes, undertaking to make, grow, develop and expand the goods and services that society desperately needs. By doing so, additional income will be generated, including tax revenues to finance government deficits.

To achieve a sustainable level of economic activity, governments around the world must spend on or invest in well-paid, highly skilled work – especially for the 73.3 million young people who were unemployed at the time of the 2015 International Labour Office survey. The ILO reports that across the world at least 197 million people are unemployed, and that this figure is set to rise by 2.3 million in 2016 and by another 1 million in 2017.[42]

Market fundamentalism – globalisation – failed catastrophically to provide meaningful work, incomes, dignity and respect to almost 200 million people in the Middle East, Africa, Latin America, parts of Asia and Europe. In the United States, globalisation has undermined the living standards of millions of working people. Market fundamentalism has also failed to prepare for or tackle the grave threats now facing a range of societies around the world. As Karl Polanyi rightly predicted in his book *The Great Transformation*, it is no wonder that populist movements gathered strength everywhere, and strong leaders were called upon to defend whole societies from the utopian but destructive predations of market fundamentalism.

Given these frightening economic and political conditions, it is urgent for *the public sector* to step in and spend: on, for example, meaningful, secure work; on transforming the economy away from fossil fuels; on addressing the challenges of both youthful and ageing populations; on re-skilling and up-skilling workforces; on higher wages for public employees; on repairing decaying infrastructure like America's pot-holed highways and energy-inefficient buildings – witness to J.K. Galbraith's 'private affluence and public squalor'.

The key to tackling the problem identified by Adair Turner – the weakness of global nominal demand – is therefore *expenditure*, specifically, public expenditure that can be undertaken quickly: on the upkeep of roads and railways, on flood defences, on water conservation, on horticulture, and so on.

Of course, public expenditure has to be financed. The most prudent form of financing is loan issuance, not 'deficit spending' which implies permanent government overdrafts. Loan issuance, arranged by the government's debt management office in concert with the central bank and fixed at low rates supported by central bank action, can finance ongoing government expenditure. Thanks to the multiplier, that expenditure on employment will quickly generate returns to the public treasury in the form of tax revenues for repayment of loans.

Furthermore, increased loan (bond or gilt) issuance managed by the central bank on the basis of liquidity preference (outlined in Chapter 3) will provide the private sector (for example, pension funds) with safe, short-, medium- and long-term assets into which capital can be invested for cash, security, or higher-risk capital gain motives. This will in turn enable the central bank to manage the spectrum of interest rates fixed by private bank clerks across private sector lending.

Government expenditure, financed by the sale of valuable, and now very scarce, government assets – bond or gilt issuance – is a democratic, transparent and accountable form of financing. It puts governments, not technocrats, firmly in the driving seat. It goes without saying that independent central bank technocrats have a duty to us all, to regulate and manage the prices and rates at which both the private and public sectors borrow money. It is for the reasons above that I consider government loan financing to be far more democratic and accountable than Overt Monetary Financing for the financing of public expenditure that alone will stimulate demand in the economy as a whole. As a consequence, it will also benefit the private sector.

Wresting power back from financial markets

Because credit (buttressed by contract law, the criminal justice system, the central bank, taxation and accounting systems) can be created with such ease, the production of credit or finance is an immense collective, public power. This power can be, and indeed has been, usurped by a small elite active in financial markets. Their power is in turn buttressed by political power as a result of the sector's influence over, and deliberate and consistent lobbying of democratic politicians and political systems.

The impact of the finance sector's power-grab for our monetary system can only be fully grasped if we compare it to a power-grab for the public sanitation system. Were the sanitation system to be captured in the same way, we would live in a world in which a small elite abused a great public good. That elite would grow fit and healthy because they would be protected from dirty water and disease, while the rest of society would be weakened by only occasional access to clean water and hygienic sanitation. That is effectively what has happened in economic terms since the finance sector made a power-grab for the money system in the late 1960s and '70s. Financial elites have grown wealthy beyond imagining; the middle classes and the poor have grown poorer as inequality has skyrocketed, and the labour movement has been shackled. This has led to economic failure, and social and political unrest.

So of course, there can be no question: money-creation powers must be wrested back from the control of this relatively small group of economic agents concentrated in financial markets on Wall Street, the City of London and Frankfurt. These markets must be made subordinate to the interests of society as a whole. If, as now, credit creation is not properly managed by and regulated on behalf of wider society, then the finance sector's hold over society will remain a divisive, destructive and despotic power. The recurring financial crises of the last four decades will roll on relentlessly and lead inevitably to graver social and political upheavals and even war.

But regaining control over the monetary system is not quite the same as returning the system to one based on a flawed understanding of money and credit. If bankers are to be stripped of their powers to issue credit, and the issuance of credit or money is to be restricted to equal the money set aside in peoples' savings, then we would quickly revert to a barter-style economy that would not be able to finance big challenges.

Fundamental to any attempt to wrest power back from financial markets must be greater public understanding of the nature of credit, money creation – and of the monetary system as a whole. Without that understanding, it will not be possible to overturn the current system. While monetary reformers have done a great deal to shed light, inform and enlighten, they may also confuse the public by re-adopting the quantity theory of money that underpins 'The Chicago Plan Revisited'. Public confusion, misunderstandings, and a flawed analysis would delay any political action to transform the system.

Worse, it would ensure that the threat posed by the present anarchic state of the global monetary and private banking system would remain unreformed, and unchanged.

CHAPTER 7

Subordinating Finance, Restoring Democracy

Socialism is, essentially, the tendency inherent in an industrial civilization to transcend the self-regulating market by consciously subordinating it to democratic society.
Karl Polanyi, *The Great Transformation*

Finance capital's 'despotic' power over the world's nations has led, since the 1970s, to a series of ongoing financial crises, and to the build-up of mountains of private, unpayable debts. These crises have inflicted grave costs – human, ecological as well as economic – on whole societies. The US Treasury estimated that 8.8 million jobs were lost in the US alone, and $19 trillion of household wealth was destroyed during the 2007–09 crisis.

But finance capital's power has done more: it has hollowed out democratic institutions, as those political powers that have the capacity to allocate resources have been privatised. The financialisation of the economy has rendered political institutions virtually powerless to represent the interests of domestic electorates. This helps explain why the costs of crises have not been borne, on the whole, by the finance sector. Most financiers were bailed out after the 2007–09 crisis. Those who have paid the price, directly or indirectly, include taxpayers, the unemployed, bankrupted small and large firms and the homeless. Western social democratic and conservative parties also paid a high price for their adoption of neoliberal policies; for attempting to separate the economic from the political sphere and for in effect colluding with finance capital against the interests of their populations. All these are costs inflicted by finance capital's unmanaged and unaccountable activities. Yet it is because of western society's subjugation to 'the yoke of ideology' that despotic power can be exercised by such a small financial elite, as Italian economists Massimo Amato and Luca Fantacci explain.[1] In other words, this is a crisis of ignorance and political impotence in the face of a set of ideas serving the interests of the few. To regain political authority over finance requires in the first instance a greater understanding of money production and of the ideological, pie-in-the-sky ideals of global financial operators. That is not easy, because so much of the private finance sector's activities are hidden, deliberately obscured from the view of economists and politicians, not to mention wider society.

By shielding its activities from public oversight and academic scrutiny, it has been possible for the finance sector to turn society's *social* construct – credit, and the social relationships between debtors and creditors – into both a false commodity and an artificial market – independent of democratic *public* authority. As part of a utopian scheme to create a single unregulated global 'shadow banking' market in credit, mobile money, trade and labour, finance capital hoped to create a parallel self-regulating planet under private authority. A planet untrammelled by human values, regulations, accountability or standards. These are values, standards and democratic institutions that societies have developed over centuries of civilising evolution. This utopian ideal – to create an autonomous parallel world of financial transactions – had been tried before, both before the First World War, when 'globalisation' ended in disaster, and after. With the re-introduction of the gold standard in the 1920s, once again 'nations and peoples were mere puppets in a show utterly beyond their control. They shielded themselves from unemployment and instability with the help of central banks ... World trade now meant organization of life on the planet under a self-regulating market, comprising labour, land and money, with the gold standard as the guardian of this gargantuan automaton.'[2]

However, the organisation of such a parallel, autonomous and 'automaton' planet was and is a delusion. Society cannot tolerate being governed by remote, unaccountable forces. Societies *will* inevitably reject the idealised, intolerable neoliberal ideal of a single, globalised market in finance, trade and labour. People will not tolerate a world in which wages are reduced, worldwide, to the lowest common denominator. A world in which one interest rate governs all economic activity, without differentiating within and between different stages of economic development in different countries. A world in which a small group of financiers has the power to decide on the allocation and price of finance. One in which technocrats, not accountable politicians, are charged with 're-structuring', 'reforming' and adjusting markets in money, labour and trade. A world in which the trading 'minnows' of the global economy are required to swim with the 'sharks' and to live with the social, economic and political consequences of being devoured by bigger fish.

We have learned from the 2007–09 crisis that without proper regulation and oversight, markets cannot buy and sell the trust (or distrust) that exists between debtors and creditors. The consequence of trying to do so is to destroy what trust exists – in money, and in financial and political institutions. The crisis proved, once again, that society's social relationships, its values and standards cannot be bought and sold like commodities, finished goods or services. They can only be upheld through the setting of democratically agreed standards, oversight and regulation.

How do we regain democratic oversight and regulation of the great public good that is our monetary system? The answer, of course, is by political means (that is, by mobilising political will and enacting legislation and regulation) to once again subordinate finance to its proper role of servicing *real* markets in goods and services.

This book cannot explore the problem of mobilising political will: that is for others far more qualified. But if societies are able to mobilise political will to hold the finance sector accountable, what policies should be adopted to subordinate finance? Below are a few easily explained but key economic policy proposals – none new or original. However, they are all tried and tested, and have proven effective in limiting the power of finance. That probably explains why they are so little discussed and examined.

Managing the production of money: macroprudential tools

Given our understanding of the 'magic' of money production by banks and other financial institutions, and given that private bankers have proven guilty of 'herd' behaviour in producing and reproducing loans, it is important for public authorities (the central bank and finance ministry or treasury) to *manage* the production and distribution of money. To be effective, money production must be managed and regulated in both the commercial and shadow banking sectors and in both the domestic and international spheres. The purpose must be to avoid booms and busts, and to ensure that finance is available to all that need it for productive purposes. In considering regulation of the finance sector, governments and taxpayers need to understand the leverage they can exercise over bankers. After all, without taxpayer guarantees and central bank largesse, most private banks would be (and some still are) insolvent. The quid pro quo for these public subsidies must be the right of central banks and democratic governments to intervene in the management of a public good: the nation's credit production system.

A guiding principle of public money production management is common sense: that privately created finance for *productive activity* should be encouraged, and priced at low rates. By contrast, money production for *speculation* should be strongly discouraged by the authorities and priced at very high rates of interest.

There is an arsenal of what are known as 'macroprudential tools' available to governments and central banks for the management of money or credit production. Governments could use these to monitor and manage credit growth, for example by monitoring and measuring private bank credit growth relative to a nation's GDP.

Another way of managing loan production is by setting standards for loan-to-value ratios. In Germany, mortgages are not offered on the *current* value of a property, as happens in the Anglo-Saxon economies. Instead, under Article 16 of the Pfandbrief Act, a prudent assessment is made on the 'long-term, permanent features of the property, normal regional market situations, as well as the present and possible alternative uses'.[3] This means that credit is not used at each purchase to constantly inflate the value of a property, so that each new buyer has to find more credit to purchase the same property, whose value, with each new credit-financed purchase, spirals upwards. Ever-rising credit creation fuels higher property prices, and lifts properties beyond the affordability of those most in need of homes. Instead, the German loan-to-value ratio is based on a longer-term assessment of the value of the property. The result is a lower valuation of German property, lower credit requirements and more stable property prices. Easy credit in Britain has been deliberately used by conservative governments to fuel the inflation of property prices and improve the so-called 'feel-good' factor. An unfortunate consequence is a shortage in the supply of affordable properties to first-time and other low-income buyers. If loan-to-valuation ratios were as cautious and balanced in the UK as they are in Germany, it is my view that there would not be the housing supply shortage so typical of London property markets.

Debt-to-income ratios and 'leverage caps' are standardised tools that central banks can require private bankers to apply – on pain of losing either their license to produce credit, or government guarantees for their customers' bank deposits.

Managing the price of money: monetary policy

Now there is no part of our economic system which works so badly as our monetary and credit arrangements; none where the results of bad working are so disastrous socially; and none where it is easier to propose a scientific solution.

J.M. Keynes, December 1923

Keynes's great contribution to monetary theory, and to the policies of his time, was based on his refutation of an important element of classical economic theory. He argued that the rate of interest was *the cause*, not as orthodox economists argued *the passive consequence*, of the level of economic activity. In other words, the level of investment, employment, and trade was caused by the rate of interest. If the rate was too high, the level of investment, employment and trade would fall. If it was low, the level of investment, employment and trade would rise.

In today's environment of low central bank rates, Keynes's argument is validated. Interest rates *appear* to be low, but that has not boosted investment. Deflation threatens. Despite low central bank rates, unemployment in large parts of the world is high (and where the unemployment rate is lower, employment is of the insecure, low-paid kind). And international trade remains subdued.

The fact is that central bank rates may be low, but they apply only to those that have accounts with central banks: bankers. Those active in the real economy – i.e. households, entrepreneurs, small and large firms – are subject to higher and rising interest rates fixed by private bank credit-risk assessors on a case-by-case basis, without any effective regulation. In its regular reports on 'Trends in Lending' and loan pricing, the Bank of England reported in 2015 that rates charged by banks to small and large firms at about 4 percent were much higher than the central bank rate of 0.5 percent.[4] While interest rates paid on customer deposits by private banks is negligible, interest on overdrafts were set at about 10 percent. For small firms, overdraft rates were much higher at about 22 percent. On one- to five-year loans, rates were at 8 percent, and on credit cards rates were in the region of 17 percent.[5]

It is those high real rates that go a long way to explaining subdued economic activity, not just in the UK, but worldwide.

At the time of writing, central banks have lowered their rates further so that for some countries rates on sovereign bonds are effectively negative. That was a bizarre development, implying that investors or lenders are paying sovereign borrowers (governments) to lend. However, the decline in inflation *raised* the real rate of interest. Contrast this with the impact of inflation on interest rates: inflation *lowers* the real rate of interest. A rising real rate of interest, brought about silently by deflationary pressures, can be expected to further depress economic activity (output and employment). Governments and central bankers were unfamiliar with the effects of deflationary pressures, and were unsure how to respond. Many foolishly welcomed falling prices as helping to boost consumption. In reality, falling prices are evidence of a fall in demand – demand for money, labour, goods and services. Indeed, their commitment to orthodox economic policies (for control of the market by the 'invisible hand' and small government) tied many governments to austerity policies which failed to boost demand and confidence. Austerity instead served to weaken the global economy, lowered demand and accelerated deflationary pressures, as countries like China built up gluts of unsold goods.

THE PRODUCTION OF MONEY

As I have outlined in Chapter 2, Keynes's theory of liquidity preference explains that interest rates, and therefore economic output and employment, can be determined and shaped by central banks managing the supply of and *demand for government assets* (i.e. government bonds/treasuries or gilts). Interest rates are not determined, as many neoclassical economists argue, by *the demand for savings*.[6]

Keynes understood that in a bank-money economy, in which society is no longer dependent on the surpluses accumulated by capitalists for credit or savings, capitalists nevertheless have to find an outlet for their surplus. They do not have any control over whether they *will* invest their surplus (they have after all to do something with their savings/ capital!) but they do have control over *the period* they are willing to invest for; the period during which they give up the ability to convert their wealth quickly into ready cash. As Dr Geoff Tily explains,

> Interest is paid not as a reward for not spending (saving) but as a reward for parting with the liquidity of wealth. Firms and governments do not need to encourage households to save to gain access to their idle resources. If firms and government are willing to borrow on liquid terms then they would not need to pay any reward for access to these resources ... Debt management policy should permit a sensible and coherent framework for the balancing of firms', governments' and households' differing preferences towards holding and borrowing wealth with different degrees of liquidity/illiquidity.[7]

So if the government wishes to determine the rate of interest and keep it low over a range of time periods, argued Keynes, then it can arrange its own borrowing, i.e. issue its own assets (debt or bonds) over time periods that suit *the liquidity preferences* of the holders of capital. Some may wish to part with capital for just one day (to be sure of cash), for thirty years (to ensure security in, for example, retirement), or for several months (in the hope of making quick, speculative gains). Vital to the control of the rate of interest, argued Keynes, is the provision of a full range of safe government assets that meet those different and varied time preferences.

Because of the government's dominant role as an issuer of bonds, the reward for parting with liquidity over different time periods can then be managed by governments through the debt management office of the finance ministry or treasury. By creating, offering and managing a range of government assets to meet the demands of investors for liquidity over different time periods, the government can both exercise greater control over its own financing costs, and also determine the rate of interest over those time periods in ways that reduce the financing costs of the private sector.

Under such sound *monetary* management, both the public and private sectors are winners.

Nevertheless, while monetary policies are important in shaping economic prosperity, they are most certainly not the whole answer. There are times, such as our own, when low rates of interest and other monetary policies are insufficient to stimulate the kind of investment needed to increase employment, improve productivity and generate income. That is when it is important for monetary policy to work hand in hand with fiscal policy. In other words, when monetary policy is like pushing on a string and the private sector is reluctant to invest and spend, then it is time for governments to initiate investment and spending – to create jobs, expand activity and income, and generate economic recovery,

Austerity leads to shortages of safe assets

Keynes understood that the rate of interest is *a social variable*, one that can be deliberately managed by the public authorities, while at the same time holding finance capital at bay.

Tily explains how Keynes directed the management of

public debt during World War II, and helped manage the rate of interest:

> During World War II the British authorities adopted a technique known as the tap issue. Under the tap system the Government issued bonds of different maturities (e.g. bills and bonds of five-year-, ten-year- and no final maturity) at pre-announced prices, but set no limits to the cash amount of any issue.
>
> The 'taps' of each bond were held open so individuals and institutions could purchase the maturity of their choice, when and to whatever quantities they desired. The system therefore enabled the public to choose the quantity of debt issued at each degree of liquidity at the price set by the Government.[8]

The suite of policies that arose from the theory established a permanent long-term rate of 3 percent on bonds set against a short-term rate on bills of 1 percent from 1933 and throughout the whole of World War II. This was an extraordinary achievement and played a significant role in Britain's ability to finance the war effort.

However, as noted earlier, Keynes's revolutionary monetary theory, his understanding of the nature of bank money, of the banking system and of how the rate of interest is determined, have since been well and truly buried by the public authorities, by the finance sector, and by mainstream academic economists. As a result, private, high real rates of interest regularly 'puncture' debt bubbles, causing them to burst and credit to 'crunch'.

Interest rates in today's bizarre global economy

By 2016, western governments had placed excessive dependence on monetary policy for lowering interest rates to kick-start recovery. Advanced economy central bankers took on all the burden of reviving economies, while governments (with the notable exception of the Chinese government) sat on their metaphorical hands.

Central bankers embarked on a policy of buying up collateral – sovereign debt – from bond markets in a process known as quantitative easing. This process of buying and then placing government debt (securities) on the balance sheets of central banks, combined with cuts in government spending, and therefore borrowing, led to a shortage of the most prized collateral: advanced countries' sovereign bonds or debt. The shortage increased the price of government bonds, and simultaneously lowered the yield (rate of return or 'interest') on these bonds. Central bankers believed they had achieved their aim of lowering interest rates on long-term bonds, and then later turned their attention to lowering yields on medium and short-term bonds.

But by this monetary-policy-only approach to kick-starting recovery, central bankers had helped cause a shortage in the bond markets of government assets, or collateral.

Collateral, like money or debt, is a critical part of the 'plumbing' of the financial system, and is used in day-to-day transactions in financial centres and for the creation of new money. Hedge funds, investment banks and other financiers use collateral to borrow and lend short-term funds, often overnight. The shortage of collateral began 'bunging up the plumbing' of the financial system in 2015. So much so that, according to Wall Street commentator David Stockman, 'some players [were] willing to lend short-term cash at a negative rate in order to get their hands on Uncle Sam's debt paper.'[9] In other words, players were willing to *pay* others to invest their cash, in exchange for safe collateral – US sovereign debt or treasuries.

A bizarre development indeed.

The radical monetary and conservative fiscal policy advocates had forced creditors and investors to either accept negative rates of interest on their investments, or to turn to other riskier assets for the purpose of creating new debt. Soon much of both the banking and the shadow banking sector's debt creation and other speculative activities were leveraged on both safe and risky collateral. There were fears that at the next 'crunch' there would be a rush for the exits as creditors/investors unwound their positions (their leverage or borrowing against an asset), and were no longer willing to accept cash but instead demand payment or repayment in the form of (a shrinking supply of) safe collateral.

How would Keynes have addressed this potential crisis? First, he would have advised the public authorities to limit the private sector's risky leveraging against scarce assets – in other words, he would have argued for regulation of risky debt-creation in the finance sector. Second, central bankers should acknowledge that some debts would never be repaid, and work with the private sector to manage the process of writing them off. Third, governments of advanced economies should begin to spend and borrow. In that way the supply of safe collateral – government debt – would expand. And given the over-indebtedness of the private sector and its lack of courage to invest, Keynes would argue that central bankers would have to work with the debt management offices of governments to issue debt at different maturities. These new debt issues would help to satisfy the finance sector's need for safe assets. In other words, central bankers should work *with* governments to manage the financial sector's 'plumbing', but also to simultaneously support government borrowing and financing at low sustainable rates. This financing via bond issues would enable governments to invest and spend to create employment and generate activity. Well-paid skilled employment would generate the income and tax revenues needed to revive the economy, and to repay private and public debts.

Yet today Keynes's advice is ignored. The results are bizarre monetary policy-making and increasingly risky developments in financial markets – threatening yet another crisis.

Managing mobile capital: the international dimension

Since 1980, cross-border investment flows have risen from 68 percent of GDP in 1980 to 438 percent of GDP in 2007, according to an expert on mobile capital Professor Hélène Rey, in a famous paper for the National Bureau of Economic Research.[10] For emerging markets, cross-border flows have gone from 35 percent to 73 percent of GDP. Professor Rey remarks that, if capital flows

> bring gains, we should be observing large effects in the data, due to the sheer scale of financial globalisation since the 1990s. There are numerous studies that try to test for effects of international capital flows on growth or on consumption volatility. Surprisingly, these effects are hard to find in macroeconomic data. As attested by the most recent surveys reviewing a long list of empirical papers, it is hard to find robust evidence of an impact of financial openness on growth or on improved risk sharing (see Eichengreen 2002; Jeanne et al. 2012; Kose et al. 2006; Obstfeld 2009) ... both on the empirical side and on the calibration side, it is so far hard to find robust support for large quantifiable benefits of international financial integration.[11]

This is an extraordinary admission from a distinguished economist, after decades in which orthodox economists and their friends in banking and media circles have extolled the virtues of mobile capital and international financial integration. Contrary to their analyses, reckless, footloose cross-border capital flows have not just failed to show benefits, they have proved largely responsible for global financial volatility and for the recurrence of financial crises.

Professor Rey is not the first to note the lack of evidence that global capital mobility brings economic benefits. Back in 1998 an equally distinguished orthodox economist, Professor Jagdish Bhagwati, argued persuasively (in a paper that has also become famous) that we had been 'bamboozled' into believing that the central pillar of globalisation – capital mobility – should be celebrated. He noted that China and Japan,

> different in politics and sociology as well as historical experience, have registered remarkable growth without capital account convertibility. Western Europe's return to prosperity was also achieved without capital account convertibility ...
>
> In short, when we penetrate the fog of implausible assertions that surrounds the case for free capital mobility we realize that the idea and the ideology of free trade and its benefits ... have been used to bamboozle us into celebrating the new world of trillions of dollars moving daily in a borderless world.[12]

Just as a well-managed banking system ends society's dependence on robber barons at home, so should a well-developed and sound banking system end society's and the economy's reliance on international, mobile capital. With a managed domestic banking system, operated in the interests of both industry and labour, then government, industry and labour need not depend on, or fear, 'bond vigilantes' or 'global capital markets'.

Our society's subjection to the predations of these markets is a tragedy entirely of our own making. We, or at least our elected representatives and public authorities, including central bankers, allowed the capital mobility genie to escape from the bottle of domestic regulation. By doing so, we, or they, were 'bamboozled' into allowing a small financial elite to create colossal quantities of private wealth while burdening the world with debt, volatility, crises and rising rates of inequality.

Somewhat belatedly, the IMF in 2016 echoed the views of Professors Rey and Bhagwati outlined above, and issued a partial mea culpa in a paper titled 'Neoliberalism: Oversold?' In it, IMF staff argued that

> the neoliberal agenda – a label used more by critics than by the architects of the policies – rests on two main planks. The first is increased competition – achieved through deregulation and the opening up of domestic markets, including financial markets, to foreign competition. The second is a smaller role for the state, achieved through privatization and limits on the ability of governments to run fiscal deficits and accumulate debt.[13]

The benefits in terms of increased growth seem fairly difficult to establish when looking at a broad group of countries, the paper argues:

> The costs in terms of increased inequality are prominent. Such costs epitomize the trade-off between the growth and equity effects of some aspects of the neoliberal agenda.
>
> Increased inequality in turn hurts the level and sustainability of growth. Even if growth is the sole or main purpose of the neoliberal agenda, advocates of that agenda still need to pay attention to the distributional effects.

None of this is news to the victims of neoliberal economic policies in many poor, heavily indebted countries, but the IMF's mea culpa rattled the cages of many a neoliberal academic and media institution. This included the venerable *Financial Times* whose economic staff attacked the IMF and 'its misplaced mea culpa for neoliberalism', declaring that by far the most important 'global economic issue is the persistent decline in productivity growth'.[14] Ironic, given that many economists regarded the decline in productivity growth as a direct consequence of mobile capital eschewing investment in productive activity in favour of speculation in volatile financial assets. A state of affairs made possible thanks to neoliberal economic policies.

Closing doors to footloose, speculative, mobile capital

Keynes understood that under a bank-money system, not only was reliance on foreign capital over but that, in order to manage the economy, countries should actually *close* their borders to footloose, mobile international capital. To do so he advocated capital control: the *taxing* of cross-border capital flows. Capital controls are taxes, and differ from exchange controls. The latter place limits on the amount of a nation's *currency* that can be taken abroad. Instead, the financial transaction tax or Tobin tax is a form of *capital* control, a tax on and 'sand in the wheels' of capital flows.

Today's excessively complex globalised financial system is very different from that of Keynes's day. But given that complexity, and given the propensity of risk assessors, CEOs and the part-time members of globalised company boards to make catastrophic errors of judgement, a sound regulatory system is now an even greater imperative. Of course capital controls are often dismissed on the grounds that they can be evaded. But then, so can taxes – and yet nobody argues for the abolition of taxes. Governments and institutions that oppose capital controls are often the very same governments that have in the past applied controls over 'hot money' as they pursued their own domestic economic goals. Now that they believe their country to be strong enough to withstand the headwinds of mobile capital, they deny those powers to the minnows of the global economy, the emerging markets and poorest countries.

Democratic policy autonomy

The argument for the management of capital flows is based on the premise that elected, democratic governments have a duty to manage the domestic economy in the interests of the population that elected them to power – and not in the interests of unaccountable, absent financiers active in global capital markets. Management of the domestic financial system and of domestic interest rates in particular will be subverted if capital is fully mobile, and lenders in international markets offer higher or lower rates beyond a country's border, rates that may not be appropriate to economic conditions in-country.

Keynes advocated controls over the mobility of capital, because 'the whole management of the domestic economy depends upon being free to have the appropriate rate of interest without reference to the rates prevailing elsewhere in the world. Capital control is a corollary to this' he wrote in a letter to R.F. Harrod in 1942. He continued:

> Freedom of capital movements is an essential part of the old laissez-faire system and assumes that it is right and desirable to have an equalisation of interest rates in all parts of the world. It assumes, that is to say, that if the rate of interest which promotes full employment in Great Britain is lower than the appropriate rate in Australia, there is no reason why this should not be allowed to lead to a situation in which the whole of British savings are invested in Australia, subject only to different estimations of risk, until the equilibrium rate in Australia has been brought down to the British rate.[15]

Removing finance's control over a nation's currency

Keynes also understood that the modern-day practice of using the rate of interest to manage the exchange rate of a currency would hurt the domestic economy, because central bankers are obliged to focus on the interests of the robber barons – international capital markets – instead of the interests of the 'makers' and exporters of the *domestic* economy. He argued that instead, central banks should manage exchange rates over a specified range *by buying and selling currency* rather than by manipulating and ratcheting up interest rates to attract *foreign* capital. This would both allow interest rate policy to be focussed on domestic interests, and at the same time, ensure stability and transparency in exchange rate arrangements.

Of course such management would require international co-operation between countries with the mutual goal of stabilising their economies. At the time of writing the Group of Eight (G8) governments appear determined to go it alone and resist any attempt at international co-ordination or co-operation.

Brexit and the need for international cooperation and coordination

International cooperation is vital for capital controls to be effective in stabilising not just domestic economies, but also the global economy. Such cooperation is, however, spurned by world leaders schooled in market fundamentalism. Rulers of the so-called 'free world' prefer to leave the international coordination of markets for money, trade and labour to the 'invisible hand'. In this sense, they resemble the feckless leaders of the 1930s who left responsibility for the global economy to the automatic, fantastical machinery of the gold standard.

The geopolitical and economic irresponsibility of today's leaders has led to predictable outcomes: stark economic imbalances; rising inequality and political tensions; threats of war between great powers; the return of nationalisms, and even fascism, in some parts of the world. Britain's Brexit vote of June 2016 revealed the growing nationalist sentiment of, in particular, older English and Welsh working class people who feel 'left behind' by globalisation.[16] This was expressed, in my view, as the urgent demand for protection from the predations caused by market fundamentalism. Immigrants are often both the victims of globalisation, and also the most tangible evidence of unfettered markets for money, trade and labour. Hostility to immigrants has grown, not just in Europe, but also in North America and Africa. These tensions clearly affirm, in my view, of the dangerous imbalances caused by unfettered flows of money, trade and labour, and of the failure of internationalism.

This decline in the spirit and intent of internationalism is reflected most clearly in divergences and tensions between two partners in the ambitious project for a peaceful, united Europe: Germany and Greece. However, tensions have intensified across the world, most notably between richer and poorer nations, and between debtor and creditor nations, as well as within nations.

As the world appears to hurtle towards an era of chaotic protectionism and the threat of war, how can democratic societies alter this disastrous course of events? I would argue that first and foremost, we must demand the transformation of our financial systems, to render the finance sector servant, not master, of both domestic economies and the global economy. The management of financial flows would begin to end the asymmetry caused by the absolute advantage that finance has enjoyed over the comparative advantages of trade and labour. (While trade and labour invariably face barriers to movement – physical, economic and political – in our globalised economy, finance faces virtually no barriers. Finance, therefore, enjoys an absolute advantage over trade and labour.)

There is a question of how to manage financial flows. Capital control, outlined above, must be one part of the approach. But for management of the international financial system as a whole, we have once again to turn to Keynes, who experienced the 1930s directly. He aimed his life's work at preventing any repetition of that era's economic slump and the catastrophic Second World War.

Keynes proposed a scheme at the 1944 Bretton Woods conference that would act as an incentive for both rich and poor countries to converge towards balance in financial, trade and labour flows. He called it an International Clearing Union (ICU). Its workings would resemble those of a domestic banking system. Just as in banking, at the heart of the ICU proposal would be the equivalent of a central bank: in this case, the master of all central banks.

The key role played by this new international central bank – the ICU – would be to manage flows of money between states, and to use a new currency, bancor, as the relevant currency. (In other words, a neutral currency, not the currency of one imperial power.) Like any other central bank (or indeed ordinary bank) the ICU would 'clear' deposits and withdrawals between trading states. And like any bank, the ICU would provide an 'overdraft' to debtor countries, enabling them to continue trading. However, it would penalise countries moving into deficit by applying punitive interest rates on that country's 'overdraft' with the ICU.

But the proposed ICU differed from other central banks in one critical respect: it would also penalise countries that built up a surplus. In other words, countries that accumulated profits from trade, and deposited those profits in the ICU would be charged punitive rates of interest on the surplus.

Keynes argued that this was necessary because imbalances – like those between indebted Greece and profitable Germany – are dangerous. They lead to economic failure for the debtor and, with it, political hostility. Adjustment to restore balance between trading nations is therefore necessary if we are to prevent trade or currency wars, but also militarised war. However, under the current system (and within the Eurozone) the adjustment to those imbalances is *compulsory* for the debtor (for instance, Greece or Mozambique), but only *voluntary* for the creditor (like Germany or the United States). If trade between nations is to be fair, and not lead to rising tensions, then it will be necessary for both the debtors like Greece, and the creditors like Germany, to manage their trade in the interests of balance and stability.

The effect of this scheme would be to force both countries to import and export less. Instead, they would focus on expanding their domestic economies, to become more self-sufficient – a framework that would reduce toxic emissions from transporting freight across the world, helping restore balance to the ecosystem, too.

We can safely assume that the finance sector hated this scheme. Why? Because global, mobile capital's absolute power derives from its ability to move effortlessly across borders and to lend at the highest rate of interest to institutions and individuals that need finance. Critically, however, this power is also dependent on repayment in hard currency. So, while finance capital is particularly keen to lend to poor countries (because 'sub-prime' lending is far more profitable) it encounters the problem of ensuring repayment. Fortunately for the global finance sector, the IMF provides protection. It does so by acting as agent on behalf of international creditors, and as gatekeeper for countries to access capital markets. Above all, the IMF enforces repayments by ensuring that debtor countries restructure and reorient their economies towards exports that earn hard currency. (International borrowers refuse to be repaid in poor countries' currencies – like the Nigerian naira, the Brazilian real or the Mozambican metical.)

Keynes's International Clearing Union would put an end to an economically and socially unjust system of international trade and finance; one that depends for financial gains on trade imbalances. The ICU is one of Keynes's greatest legacies. As Edward Harrison has argued, 'it would use market forces to create greater symmetry in the incentives for both debtors and creditors to end imbalances.'[17] Sadly, the idea was dismissed by the rising power of the time, the United States, before it could be tried.

The restoration of the ICU is vital if societies are to overcome the ideology of market fundamentalism and restore balance, stability, and above all, peace to the world.

A suite of policies for subordinating finance to the real economy

Most of the suite of policies briefly outlined above led to proven economic success during the period of 1945–71. Over this period, and in the interest of their own people, governments managed credit creation, interest rates across the spectrum of lending, mobile capital and the exchange rate. This movement away from the financial anarchy of the 1920s to management of the finance sector gradually loosened the control wealthy elites had over the financial system and the economy. Management of finance was the underlying principle of the Bretton Woods financial architecture for its duration (1945–70) which was and still is defined as the Golden Age of economics. These policies in turn loosened finance capital's control over society, and over democratic institutions. The power, status and prestige of bankers in Britain and the United States was considerably modified. The period was one the famous historians Eichengreen and Lindert described as, 'a golden era of tranquillity in international capital markets, a fulfilment of the benediction "May you live in dull times."'[18]

Keynesian *monetary* policies managed the banking system in support of the government's fiscal policy, and in the interests of society as a whole, ensuring that all major stakeholders in the economy enjoyed a share of a bigger cake.

However, soon after Keynes's death, his theory and its practical application began to be neglected or discredited by, you guessed it, the finance sector and their friends in the economics profession. In its place the Hayekian (neoliberal) and so-called 'Keynesian' schools of economics restored the old classical theory. This once again asserted that savings are needed for investment, that bankers are mere intermediaries between savers and borrowers, etc. Above all, the classical theory elevates the role of finance capital and capital markets in the lending markets, and restores to private wealth the power to determine interest rates. It is a collection of plausible fantasies – an ideology – that has enriched the already rich, and systematically replaced more democratic policies and financial management.

In other words, by removing the policies and regulations that allowed governments to manage the economy, orthodox economists restored to finance capital the power it had exercised before the stock market crash of 1929. Power, then as now, resided not only with those who had amassed great wealth but also with those who could make new gains through lending. By obfuscating the nature of their business, bankers have established a new kind despotism.

Today central bankers retain a tenuous hold over the 'short', 'policy' or 'base' rate charged to banks (and not to other borrowers), but do not exercise influence or control over the full spectrum of interest rates. These are fixed by 'the market'. As a result, rates on the whole spectrum of lending are socially constructed – fixed or manipulated – by finance capital's minions, by 'submitters' in the back offices of banks like Barclays, and by banking cartels such as the British Banking Association.

They are not fixed to suit the wider interests of industry or labour.

Neoliberal theorists and practitioners (like Jens Weidmann and Otmar Issing, respectively president and former chief economist of the Bundesbank) while aware of the nature of credit creation, appear to have little understanding of bank money, and deliberately ignore the role of commercial banks in credit creation.[19] The effect of this blind spot concedes and reinforces finance capital's power. That helps explain why the neoliberal economic policies of the German Bundesbank and the European Central Bank placed Eurozone economies at the mercy of the unfettered speculation of capital markets, their risky lending (to, for example, Greece) and their usurious rates of interest.

There are differences though. Today's robber barons enjoy eye-popping stocks of wealth that are historically unprecedented. And the rates of interest they demand for parting with this wealth make the usurious practices of the money-lenders of the past seem modest.

Keynes's *fiscal* policies for full employment and for recovery from financial crisis have since been presented as his sole outstanding legacy – isolated from *The General Theory of Employment, Interest and Money*. This campaign was part of a wider effort by finance capital to undermine our democracy. A renewed appreciation of Keynes's legacy will not be sufficient to break the power of finance, but it is certainly necessary.

CHAPTER 8

Yes, We *Can* Afford What We Can Do

How can we restore to our democracy the public good that is the modern banking system? And how can we avoid the confiscation of this public good in the future as we deal with the threat of climate change and energy insecurity?

The answers I would suggest are as follows. First, the public must develop a much greater understanding of how the bank money system works. Knowledge is both powerful and empowering. Today's dominant flawed economic ideology will be weakened by wider public understanding of the financial system. Sadly, we cannot look to our universities for greater understanding. Departments of economics are overwhelmingly staffed by 'classical' or 'neoclassical' economists. These have no firm foundation in monetary theory on which to develop appropriate policies. Furthermore, university departments are packed with microeconomists who study economic processes in detail, and often in isolation, and then wrongly draw macroeconomic conclusions from such processes.

Stephen Cecchetti, at a workshop organised by the Bank of International Settlements in May 2012 highlighted a key flaw at the heart of most microeconomic modelling:

> Let's say that we are trying to measure tide height at the beach. We know that the sea is filled with fish, and so we exhaustively model fish behaviour, developing complex models of their movements and interactions ... The model is great. And the model is useless. The behaviour of the fish is irrelevant for the question we are interested in: how high will the seawater

go up the beach? ... By building microeconomic foundations we are focusing on the fish when we should be studying the moon.[1]

Microeconomic models are great, but for our purposes, they are useless. It is no wonder that most mainstream academic economists could not answer the Queen's famous question, 'Why was the crisis not predicted?' Their models had missed entirely the deluge that beached many banks and other financial institutions in 2007–09.

As the global financial crisis rolls on around the world, and economic failure intensifies, many economists remain detached from policy debates that could help stabilise the global economy and alleviate human suffering. And many still do not understand how the private banking system created debts vast as space with which to crash the economy. Central bankers – the 'guardians of the nation's finances' – have also surrendered to defeatism and given up on any effort to re-structure the global banking system. *Financial Times* correspondent Robin Harding filed this depressing report after the 2013 annual gathering of the world's central bankers in Jackson Hole, Wyoming:

> The world is doomed to an endless cycle of bubble, financial crisis and currency collapse. Get used to it. At least, that is what the world's central bankers – who gathered in all their wonky majesty last week for the Federal Reserve Bank of Kansas City's annual conference in Jackson Hole, Wyoming – seem to expect.
>
> All their discussion of the international financial system was marked by a fatalist acceptance of the status quo. Despite the success of unconventional monetary policy and recent big upgrades to financial regulation, we still have no way to tackle imbalances in the global economy, and that means new crises in the future.[2]

If the people lead, the leaders will follow

Given the defeatism of our leaders, it is imperative that the people lead. In particular, there are two overlapping groups in society whose engagement in these issues is vital. If they take the lead in debates about the monetary system, the need to bring offshore capitalism onshore, the management of credit creation, and the management and pricing of credit, they will stand a much better chance of securing their objectives.

The first are women; the second, environmentalists.

For women the issue is central because, first, while women are largely responsible for managing household budgets, they have on the whole been excluded from managing the nation's financial system and its budgets. Thankfully this is changing with the appointment of women to critically important posts within the economy. However, women students, working women, the members of Mumsnet, business women, all largely stand on the sidelines of debate about monetary theory and policy. At present the networks that dominate the financial sector are overwhelmingly male, and often shockingly sexist. Their dismissive attitude towards half the population and their enjoyment of an unequal distribution of knowledge are not coincidental. They are part of the same despotism that harms the great majority, male and female, and that feminism is uniquely well placed to challenge. If nothing else, feminists should want to challenge the friends of finance every time they utter the phrase 'any housewife will tell you that you can't spend money you don't have'. I hope I have shown that this is nothing more than a ruse to obscure the realities of credit creation and to enlist prudent women of modest means to support policies that serve the interests of wealthy and reckless men.

Secondly, the refrain 'there is no money' most frequently applies to women's interests and causes. While there is enough money to bail out bankers, there is never enough money to fund all the social services women provide to society. There is never enough money to reduce high rates of maternal and newborn mortality across the world; to pay fair and decent wages to women and to provide adequate and high quality childcare for women at work. The creation and management of society's money does not currently loom large in contemporary feminism. But it *is* a feminist issue, and is central to the liberation of women from the servitude of unpaid work.

The second group that stands to benefit from engaging in the issues raised by the management of the monetary system are environmentalists. It is my contention that there is a direct link between the deregulated, uncontrolled expansion of credit, increased consumption and rising greenhouse gases. By isolating consumption from the creation of credit, environmentalists are fighting a losing cause. By failing to understand how 'easy money' finances 'easy consumption' and with it rising toxic emissions, eco warriors are missing a trick. By failing to understand that repayments on high levels of expensive debt lead to and demand increasing exploitation of the earth's scarce and precious resources, environmentalists will fail to check rising greenhouse gases and the depletion and extinction of species. The link between liberal finance and increased exploitation of the ecosystem is strong: to protect the ecosystem, it is vital to first manage and regulate finance.

But to be armed with knowledge and understanding is not enough. We must go further. We must reinvigorate our political and democratic institutions because they are the vehicles by which society collectively and democratically agrees to legislative and regulatory change. We must understand that if our democratic institutions have been hollowed out by liberalisation and privatisations; if our politicians have been co-opted or captured, stripped of policy-making powers and of the power to allocate resources, then that is not accidental but the deliberate result of finance capital's actions, its lobbying and its consequent power over us all. To challenge finance, it is essential that we engage in, rebuild and strengthen democratic political parties and institutions; that we participate in political debate and in elections, and in loud, open discussion about issues that have a profound impact on our lives.

In other words, we, the people, have to organise; and to be clear about the financial and economic transformation we aim for in order to bring about a more ecologically sustainable world.

I have long believed that an alliance between labour and industry is important if finance is to be effectively challenged. The interests of both would be served by subordinating finance to its proper role as servant not master of the real, productive economy. Some argue that the financialisation of industry makes such an alliance impossible. I am not so sure. There are makers and creators out there who resent the bullying of financiers and the costs of rentier capitalism as much as any trade unionist or activist.

As to the policies needed to subdue finance capital, these are known, and have been briefly outlined in the previous chapter. We do not have to reinvent the wheel. We do not need a social revolution. We simply have to reclaim knowledge and understanding of money and finance – knowledge that has been available to society for many centuries. We need to reform and adjust monetary policy. We need to bring offshore capitalism back onshore. We *can* turn the clock back *and* move forward. Of course finance and their friends in the media, the universities and the establishment will resist, because monetary reform is the thing they fear most – far more than the revolts and occupations of city squares by ordinary citizens. Protest without concrete proposals for policy changes, and indeed for a transformation, pose no threat to the invisible, intangible global financial system.

If we cannot, through sensible monetary reform, dismantle finance capital's great power then it is my fear that society will react to the immiseration of unpayable debts, unemployment and falling incomes in ways that will be politically ugly, chaotic and destructive.

But it need not be this way. I have tried, in this short book, to explain that for those privileged enough to live in societies with a developed banking system and with the public institutions needed to uphold the integrity of the banks, there need never be a shortage of finance.

With sound monetary policies in place, we can ensure that society has the finance it needs to transform the economy away from its dependence on fossil fuels and towards more sustainable forms of energy. Because there need never be a shortage of finance, we can afford to undertake this huge transformation *and* care for the ageing population, the young and the vulnerable. We can surely afford great works of art and music. In short, we can afford all those things we can do, within the limits imposed by human shortcomings and by the ecosystem.

But that great transformation can only happen if we the people equip ourselves with a full and proper understanding of mobile capital, money creation, bank money and interest rates – and then begin to demand the reform and restoration of a just monetary system, one that makes finance servant to the economy and removes it from its current role as master.

With an understanding of what constitutes just money, a monetary system that meets all of society's needs, we – as women, environmentalists, trades unionists, producers, creators, businessmen and women, designers, activists, farmers – can lead our leaders into once again doing the right thing. Namely, adopting straightforward and well-understood monetary reforms that will bring offshore capitalism back onshore, and break the despotic power that finance capital exercises over us all.

Acknowledgements

I am heavily indebted to Dr Geoff Tily, senior economist at the British TUC, and author of *Keynes's General Theory, the Rate of Interest and 'Keynesian' Economics* (Palgrave, 2007); and of the re-print *Keynes Betrayed* (Palgrave, 2010). Geoff has generously shared his wide knowledge of Keynes and of monetary theory and policy, pointed me in the direction of experts and scholarship, and has always done so with patience, wit and charm. However, he cannot be held responsible for any of the contents of this book. Many others have illuminated the murkier corners of monetary theory and policy for me, including Professor Victoria Chick, Professor Steve Keen and my colleagues at the New Economics Foundation, Tony Greenham and Josh Ryan-Collins. Mary Mellor, Margrit Kennedy, Susan Strange and Yves Smith have all helped shape and form my thinking, and I am immensely grateful to them for that. I owe a particular debt to Geoffrey Ingham, author of *The Nature of Money* (Polity Press, 2004), a book very important to me because of its clear and forensic analysis of money and the monetary system.

I owe unpayable debts to my husband and best friend Jeremy Smith. He has been and remains the wind beneath my increasingly ragged wings. Finally, sincere thanks are due to Rachel Calder, my agent, and Dan Hind, my patient editor, and to Leo Hollis, my publisher at Verso. They have believed in me, and in the book, and that confidence is a gift for any author.

Notes

Preface

1   Mohamed El-Erian in 'The Lehman Crisis: One Year Later', *Fortune*, 28 September 2009.
2   Richard Dobbs, Susan Lund, Jonathan Woetzel and Mina Mutafchieva, 'Debt and (Not Much) Deleveraging', *McKinsey Global Institute*, February 2015, mckinsey.com, accessed 5 June 2016.
3   *New York Times* editorial, 'The Millions Who Are Just Getting By', *New York Times*, 2 June 2016, nytimes.com, accessed 5 June 2016.
4   Rich Miller, 'Risky Reprise of Debt Binge Stars US Companies Not Consumers', *Bloomberg*, 31 May 2016, bloomberg.com, accessed 5 June 2016.
5   Emily Cadman, 'Osborne Welcomes Right Kind of Deflation as Good News for Families', *Financial Times*, 20 May 2015.
6   OECD, 'Policymakers: Act Now to Keep Promises!', *Economic Outlook No. 99*, 1 June 2016, oecd.org, accessed 5 June 2016.
7   Steve Keen, *Debunking Economics, Revised and Expanded Edition: The Naked Emperor Dethroned?* London: Zed Books, 2001, p. xiii.
8   Darren K. Carlson, *Americans Weigh In on Evolution vs. Creationism in Schools*, 2005, gallup.com, accessed 8 June 2016.
9   John Maynard Keynes, *Economic Possibilities for our Grandchildren*, 1930, econ.yale.edu.

1. Credit Power

1   Michael Hudsen, *Killing the Host: How Financial Parasites and Debt Bondage Destroy the Global Economy*, New York: Nation Books, 2016.
2   Geoffrey Ingham, *The Nature of Money*, Cambridge: Polity Press, 2004.
3   Sir Mervyn King in an interview with Martin Wolf, 'Lunch with the *FT*', *Financial Times*, 14 June 2013, ft.com, accessed 6 June 2016.

And the thing that's so extraordinary is that, for the past few years, the banking system, which is normally responsible for creating 95 percent of broad money has been contracting its part of the money supply. And since we at the bank only supply about 5 percent of it, the proportional increase in our bit has to be massive to offset the contraction of the rest.

4 See Cullen Roche, 'Understanding Why Austrian Economics Is Flawed', *Pragmatic Capitalism,* 10 September 2013, pragcap. com, accessed 3 October 2013.

5 For more on this, see William Keegan, *Mrs Thatcher's Economic Experiment,* London: Penguin Books, 1984.

6 Ibid., p. 208.

7 Jon Ward, 'He Found the Flaw?' verbatim report in the *Washington Times,* 24 October 2008, washingtontimes.com, accessed 6 June 2016.

8 Gillian Tett, 'Silos and Silences – Why So Few People Spotted the Problems in Complex Credit and What This Implies for the Future', *Financial Stability Review,* No. 14, Paris: Banque de France, July 2010, banque-france.fr, accessed 3 October 2013.

9 Karl Polanyi, *The Great Transformation: The Political and Economic Origins of Our Time,* Boston: Beacon Press, 1957, p. 217.

2. The Creation of Money

1 Polanyi, *The Great Transformation,* p. 132.

2 Joseph Schumpeter, *A History of Economic Analysis,* Oxford: Oxford University Press, 1954, pp. 114–15.

3 John Law, *Money and Trade Considered with a Proposal for Supplying the Nation with Money,* 1705, avalon.law.yale.edu, accessed 6 June 2016.

4 Andrea Terzi, 'The Eurozone Crisis: A Debt Shortage as the Final Cause', INET Annual Conference, *New Economic Thinking: Liberté, Égalité, Fragilité,* Paris, 8–11 April 2015. Emphases mine.

5 John Maynard Keynes, 'National Self-Sufficiency', *The Yale Review,* Vol. 22(4), June 1933, pp. 755–69, mtholyoke.edu, accessed 6 June 2016.

6 Michael McLeay, Amar Radia and Ryland Thomas, 'Money in the Modern Economy: An Introduction and Money Creation in the Modern Economy', *Bank of England Quarterly Bulletin,* Vol. 54(1), 2014, bankofengland.co.uk, accessed 6 June 2016.

7   John Maynard Keynes, *The Collected Writings, A Treatise on Money: The Pure Theory of Money*, Vol. 5, Cambridge: Cambridge University Press, 2012 (1930).

8   Andy Haldane speech, 'The $100 Billion Question', *Bank of England*, March 2010, bankofengland.co.uk, 7 June 2016.

9   Laura E. Kodres, 'What Is Shadow Banking', in IMF publication *Finance and Development*, June 2013, Vol. 50, No. 2, imf.org.

10   Alan Greenspan speech, 'Remarks by Chairman Alan Greenspan', American Bankers Association Annual Convention, 5 October 2004, New York, federalreserve.gov, accessed 6 June 2016.

11   Mark Carney speech, 'Fortune Favours the Bold', Lecture to Honour the Memory of The Honourable James Michael Flaherty, 28 January 2015, Dublin, bankofengland.co.uk, accessed 6 June 2016.

3. The 'Price' of Money

1   This section draws on Geoff Tily, *Keynes Betrayed*, London: Palgrave Macmillan, 2010.

2   Charles R. Geisst, *Beggar thy Neighbour: A History of Usury and Debt*, Philadelphia: University of Pennsylvania Press, 2013, p. 7.

3   J. Martin Hattersley, 'Committee on Monetary and Economic Reform, Frederick Soddy and the Doctrine of "Virtual Wealth"', Fourteenth Annual Convention of the Eastern Economics Association, 1988, nesara.org, accessed 30 September 2013.

4   I am indebted to Margrit Kennedy for use of this chart. Margrit Kennedy, *Interest and Inflation Free Money*, Michigan: Seva International, 1995, kennedy-bibliothek.info, accessed 30 September 2013.

5   Duncan Needham, *UK Monetary Policy from Devaluation to Thatcher, 1967–82*, London: Palgrave Macmillan, 2014, p. 3.

6   I am grateful to Dr Graham Gudgin of Cambridge University for his insights into this period.

7   See Costas Lapavistas, *Profiting Without Producing: How Finance Exploits Us All*, London: Verso Books, 2013.

8   'The LIBOR Scandal: The Rotten Heart of Finance', *The Economist*, 7 July 2012.

9   Geoff Tily, 'Keynes's Monetary Theory of Interest' in *Threat of Fiscal Dominance?*, Bank for International Settlements, Paper No. 65, May 2012, bis.org, accessed 25 March 2014.

10   Tily, *Keynes Betrayed*, p. 184.

4. The Mess We're In

1 Margaret Thatcher speech to the Conservative Party, October 1983, margaretthatcher.org/document/105454, accessed 1 October 2013.

2 Bernie Sanders, 'Federal Reserve System: Opportunities Exist to Strengthen Policies and Processes for Managing Emergency Assistance', US Government Accountability Office, July 2011, sanders.senate.gov, accessed 4 October 2013.

3 Mervyn King speech, cited in 'BoE Governor Signals Fragile UK Recovery', Sky News, 21 October 2009, news.sky.com, accessed 4 October 2013.

4 Mervyn King speech to Scottish Business Organisations, Edinburgh, 20 October 2009.

5 Liam Byrne quoted in Paul Owen, 'Ex-Treasury Secretary Liam Byrne's Note to His Successor: There's No Money Left', *Guardian*, 17 May 2010, theguardian.com, accessed 4 October 2011.

6 Rowena Mason, 'George Osborne: UK Has Run Out of Money', *Daily Telegraph*, 27 February 2012, telegraph.co.uk, accessed 4 October 2013.

7 Ed Balls speech, 'Striking the Right Balance for the British Economy', Thomson Reuters, 3 June 2013, labour.org.uk, accessed 4 October 2013.

8 Jeremy Warner, 'Oh God – I Cannot Take Any More of the Austerity Debate', *Daily Telegraph* blog, 11 September 2013, telegraph.co.uk, accessed 3 October 2013.

9 Adam Kucharski, 'Betting and Investment Both Require Skill and Luck', *Financial Times*, 5 May 2016, ft.com, accessed 1 September 2016.

10 OECD, 'Stronger Growth Remains Elusive: Urgent Policy Response Is Needed', *Interim Economic Outlook*, 18 February 2016, oecd.org, accessed 6 June 2016.

11 Richard Koo cited in 'Quantitative Easing, the Greatest Monetary Non-Event', *Pragmatic Capitalism*, 9 August 2010, pragcap.com, accessed 3 October 2013. My emphasis.

12 The following paragraphs are drawn from the second report of the Green New Deal of which Ann Pettifor was a co-author. The Green New Deal Group, 'The Cuts Won't Work', *New Economics Foundation*, 7 December 2009, greennewdealgroup .org, accessed 25 March 2014.

13 Olivier Blanchard and Daniel Leigh, 'Growth Forecast Errors and Fiscal Multipliers', IMF Working Paper, January 2013, imf. org, accessed 6 June 2016.

14 John Maynard Keynes, *The Means to Prosperity,* London: Macmillan, 1933. Published in John Maynard Keynes, *Essays in Persuasion,* The Royal Economic Society, 1972, p. 335.

15 Eric Platt and Jo Rennison, 'US Stock Funds Suffer $11bn Outflows – Redemptions Since the Beginning of the Year Top $60bn', *Financial Times,* 6 May 2016, ft.com, accessed 6 June 2016.

16 Hoisington Investment Management Company, *Quarterly Review and Outlook: First Quarter 2016,* hoisingtonmgt.com, accessed 6 June 2016.

17 Transcript of Eric Holder to the Senate Judiciary Committee, 'Attorney General Eric Holder on "Too Big to Jail"', *American Banker,* 6 March 2013, americanbanker.com, accessed 3 October 2013.

18 Wolfgang Münchau, 'Europe Is Ignoring the Scale of Bank Losses', *Financial Times,* 23 June 2013, ft.com, accessed 17 September 2013.

5. Class Interests and the Moulding of Schools of Economic Thought

1 This chapter is based on the paper *What Are the Economic Possibilities for Our Grandchildren?* drafted in collaboration with Dr Geoff Tily. It was delivered in Cambridge on 16 November 2015 by the author as one of the events organised by King's College's Politics Society to celebrate the five-hundredth anniversary of the completion of the stonework of King's College Chapel.

2 Mervyn King speech, 'Twenty Years of Inflation Targeting', Stamp Memorial Lecture, London School of Economics, 9 October 2012.

3 P. Samuelson, *Economics*, 9th ed., New York: McGraw-Hill, 1973, quoted in Geoffrey Ingham, *The Nature of Money*, Cambridge: Polity Press, 2004, p. 15. My emphasis.

4 Joseph Vogl, 'Sovereignty Effects', INET Conference Berlin, 12 April 2012, ineteconomics.org, accessed 6 June 2016.

5 Michael McLeay, Amar Radia and Ryland Thomas, 'Money in the Modern Economy: An Introduction' and 'Money Creation in the Modern Economy', *Bank of England Quarterly Bulletin* Vol. 54(1), 2014, bankofengland.co.uk, accessed 6 June 2016.

6 John Hobson, *Imperialism: A Study*, London: James Nisbet & Co., 1902, pp. 218–19. My emphasis.

7   C.A.E. Goodhart, 'The Continuing Muddles of Monetary Theory: A Steadfast Refusal to Face Facts', boeckler.de, accessed 6 June 2016.

8   Keynes, *The Collected Writings*, Vol. 5.

9   Mark Carney speech 'One Mission. One Bank. Promoting the Good of the People of the United Kingdom', Mais Lecture at Cass Business School, bankofengland.co.uk, accessed 6 June 2016.

10 John Maynard Keynes, *The General Theory of Employment, Interest and Money*, 1936, marxists.org, accessed 6 June 2016.

11 Josh Ryan Collins, Tony Greenham, Richard Werner and Andrew Jackson, *Where Does Money Come From?* London: New Economics Foundation, 2011.

12 Keynes cited in Geoff Tily *Keynes's General Theory, the Rate of Interest and 'Keynesian' Economics,* London: Palgrave Macmillan, 2007, p. 71.

13 David Smith, *From Boom to Bust,* London: Penguin Group, 1992, p. 5.

14 Ibid., p. 6.

15 For more on 1960s policies for 'growth' see Geoff Tily, 'The National Accounts, GDP and the "Growthmen"', 2015, primeeconomics.org, accessed 9 June 2016.

6. Should Society Strip Banks of the Power to Create Money?

1   Mary Mellor, *Debt or Democracy*: *Public Money for Sustainability and Social Justice*, London: Pluto Press, 2016.

2   Martin Wolf, *The Shifts and the Shocks: What We've Learned – and Have Still to Learn – from the Financial Crisis*, London: Penguin, 2015.

3   See Robert N. Proctor and Londa Schievinger, *Agnotology: The Making and Unmaking of Ignorance*, California: Stanford University Press, 2008.

4   Antoine E. Murphy, *John Law, Economic Theorist and Policy-Maker,* Oxford: Clarendon Press, 1997, p. 51.

5   Mellor, *Debt,* p. 13.

6   'Creating a Sovereign Monetary System', *Positive Money*, 2014, positivemoney.org, accessed 2 June 2016, p. 8.

7   Mellor, *Debt,* p. 69.

8   Ibid.

9   Joseph Huber, 'Sovereign Money in Critical Context: Explaining Monetary Reform by Using Typical Misunderstandings',

Positive Money, 2014, positivemoney.org, accessed 2 June 2016.

10 John Maynard Keynes, 'An Open Letter to President Roosevelt', 1933, newdeal.feri.org, accessed 2 June 2016.

11 As explained in Jaromir Benes and Michael Kumhof, 'The Chicago Plan Revisited', IMF Working Paper, August 2012, imf.org, accessed 6 June 2016.

12 Ibid.

13 Ibid., p. 6.

14 Ibid.

15 Ibid., p. 5.

16 Ibid., p. 13.

17 David Smith, *The Rise and Fall of Monetarism*, London: Penguin Books, 1987, p. 13.

18 Ibid., p. 19.

19 Ibid., p. 37.

20 Professor Wynne Godley, in Chapter 19 of Ann Pettifor ed., *Real World Economic Outlook*, London: New Economics Foundation and Palgrave MacMillan, 2003, p. 178. My emphasis.

21 Ben Dyson, Andrew Jackson, Graham Hodgson, 'Creating A Sovereign Monetary System', 15 July 2014, positivemoney.org, accessed 10 June 2016.

22 David Graeber, *Debt: The First 5,000 Years*, New York: Melville House Press, 2011.

23 Ibid., p. 76.

24 Izabella Kaminska, 'When Memory Becomes Money; The Story of Bitcoin so far', *Financial Times* blog, ftalphaville. ft.com, accessed 3 April, 2013.

25 Friedrich A. Hayek, *Denationalisation of Money: The Argument Refined*, London: The Institute of Economic Affairs, 1990.

26 Jonathan Levin, *'Governments will struggle to put Bitcoin under lock and key'*, *The Conversation*, theconservation.com, accessed 27 November, 2013

27 Izabella Kaminska, *'How I learned to stop blockchain obsessing and love the Barry Manilow'*, *Financial Times* blog, ftalphaville.ft.com, accessed 10 August, 2016.

28 Izabella Kaminska, *'Day three post Bitfinex hack: Bitcoin bailouts, liabilities and hard forks'*, *Financial Times* blog, ftalphaville.ft.com, accessed 12 October, 2016.

29 A short Google search reveals that one cosmetic surgery company offers rates of 16.9 percent on loans to finance a 'transformation' in one's looks, transforminglives.co.uk, accessed 6 June 16.

30 See Ulrich Bindseil, *Monetary Policy Operations and the Financial System*, Oxford: Oxford University Press, 2014, p. 84.

31 The Federal Reserve Bank of Minneapolis, *Discovering Open Market Operations*, 1 August 1988, minneapolisfed.org, accessed 2 June 2016.

32 Frank van Lerven, 'A Guide to Public Money Creation', Positive Money, May 2016, positivemoney.org, accessed 2 June 2016.

33 Ibid., p. 19.

34 Ibid., p. 22. My emphasis.

35 Ibid., p 23. My emphasis.

36 Ibid., p. 27.

37 Adair Turner, 'Helicopters on a Leash', *Project Syndicate*, 9 May 2016, project-syndicate.org, accessed 2 June 2016.

38 Ibid., pp. 2–4.

39 From Keynes, 'An Open Letter to President Roosevelt'. My emphasis.

40 Adair Turner, 'Helicopters on a Leash', *Project Syndicate*, 9 May 2016, project-syndicate.org, accessed 26 July 2016.

41 Quoted in Martin Wolf, 'George Osborne's Desire to Cut Spending Makes Little Sense', *Financial Times,* 4 March 2016.

42 International Labour Office, *World Employment and Social Outlook: Trends 2016*, January 2016, ilo.org, accessed 2 June 2016.

7. Subordinating Finance, Restoring Democracy

1 Massimo Amato and Luca Fantacci, *The End of Finance,* Cambridge: Polity Press, 2011.

2 Polanyi, *The Great Transformation*, p. 217.

3 Paul Trott, '2009 EMF Study on the Valuation of Property for Lending Purposes', European Mortgage Federation, November 2009, law.berkeley.edu, accessed 2 June 2016.

4 Bank of England, 'Trends in Lending: April 2015', bankofengland.co.uk, accessed 2 June 2016.

5 Chart G1.1, 'Bankstats (Monetary and Financial Statistics)', Bank of England, March 2016, bankofengland.co.uk, accessed 2 June 2016.

6 For a detailed exposition of Keynes's liquidity preference theory, see Tily, *Keynes Betrayed*, Chapter 7.

7 Ibid.

8 Ibid., p. 202.

9 David Stockman 'How The Fed Turned a Flood of Treasury Debt into a Scarcity of Repo Collateral', *David Stockman's Contra*

Corner, 14 August 2014, davidstockmanscontracorner.com, accessed on 2 June 2016.

10   Hélène Rey, 'Dilemma Not Trilemma: The Global Financial Cycle and Monetary Policy Independence', National Bureau of Economic Research, May 2015, nber.org, accessed 2 June 2016, p. 311.

11   Ibid.

12   Jagdish Bhagwati, 'The Capital Myth: The Difference Between Trade in Widgets and Dollars', *Foreign Affairs*, Vol. 3, No. 77, May/June 1998.

13   Jonathan D. Ostry, Prakash Loungani and Davide Furceri, 'Neoliberalism: Oversold?', *Finance and Development* Vol. 53, No. 2, June 2016, imf.org, accessed 2 June 2016.

14   *Financial Times* editorial, 'A Misplaced Mea Culpa for Neoliberalism', *Financial Times,* 30 May 2016, ft.com, accessed 2 June 2016.

15   John Maynard Keynes to R. F. Harrod, 19 April 1942, in John Maynard Keynes, *Collected Writings*, Vol. 25, Cambridge: Cambridge University Press, 2012, pp. 148–9.

16   For more on this see Lord Ashcroft Polls, 'How the United Kingdom Voted on Thursday, and Why', 24 June, 2016, lordashcroftpolls.com, accessed 13 October 2016.

17   Edward Harrison, 'The German Current Account Surplus Requires Deficits Elsewhere,' primeeconomics.org, 11 May, 2016 accessed 13 October 2016.

18   Barry Eichengreen and Peter H. Lindert, *The International Debt Crisis in Historical Perspective,* Cambridge: MIT Press, 1991, p. 1.

19   Norbert Häring, 'The Veil of Deception over Money: How Central Bankers and Textbooks Distort the Nature of Banking and Central Banking', *Real-World Economics Review*, No. 63, 2013, paecon.net, accessed 1 October 2013.

8.   Yes, We *Can* Afford What We Can Do

1   Stephen Cecchetti, 'Comment' in 'Threat of Fiscal Dominance?' *Bank for International Settlements*, Paper No. 65, 2013, bis. org, accessed 4 October 2013.

2   Robin Harding, 'Central Bankers Have Given Up on Fixing Global Finance', *Financial Times*, 27 August 2013, ft.com, accessed 3 October 2013.

Recommended Reading List

Amato, Massimo and Luca Fantacci, *The End of Finance,* Cambridge: Polity Press, 2011.

Akyüz, Yilmaz, *Financial Crisis and Global Imbalances: A Development Perspective*, Geneva: The South Centre, 2012.

Chick, Victoria, *The Theory of Monetary Policy* (Revised Edition), Oxford: Parkgate Books in association with Basil Blackwell, 1977.

Galbraith, J.K., *Money: Whence It Came, Where It Went,* London: Penguin Books, 1975.

Greenham, Tony, and Andrew Jackson, John Ryan-Collins, Richard Werner, *Where Does Money Come From?* (Second Edition), London: New Economics Foundation, 2012.

Helleiner, Eric, *States and the Re-emergence of Global Finance*. Ithaca, NY: Cornell University Press, 1994.

Ingham, Geoffrey, *The Nature of Money*, Cambridge: Polity Press, 2004.

Keen, Steven, *Debunking Economics – Revised and Expanded Edition: The Naked Emperor Dethroned?* London: Zed Books, 2011.

Kennedy, Margrit, *Interest and Inflation Free Money*, Michigan: Seva International, 1995.

Keynes, John Maynard, *The General Theory of Employment, Interest and Money*, Cambridge: Cambridge University Press, 1973.

Lapavitsas, Costas, *Profiting Without Producing: How Finance Exploits Us All,* London: Verso Books, 2013.

Mazzucato, Mariana, *The Entrepreneurial State: Debunking Public versus Private Sector Myths*, London: Anthem Press, 2013.

Mellor, Mary, *The Future of Money: From Financial Crises to Public Resource*, London: Pluto Press, 2010.

Polanyi, Karl, *The Great Transformation: The Political and Economic Origins of Our Time*, Boston: Beacon Press, 1957.

Strange, Susan, *Mad Money: When Markets Outgrow Government*, Manchester: Manchester University Press, 1998.

Tily, Geoff, *Keynes Betrayed: Keynes's General Theory, the Rate of Interest and 'Keynesian' Economics*, London: Palgrave Macmillan, 2007.

Other relevant reading

Cockett, Richard, *Thinking the Unthinkable*, London: Harper Collins Publishers, 1994.

Daly, H.E., *Economics, Ecology, Ethics*, San Francisco: W.H. Freeman & Co., 1973.

Daly, H.E., *Steady-State Economics*, San Francisco: W. H. Freeman & Co., 1977.

Elliott, Larry and Colin Hines, Tony Juniper, Jeremy Leggett, Caroline Lucas, Richard Murphy, Ann Pettifor, Charles Secrett, Andrew Simms, *A Green New Deal*, London: Green New Deal Group, 2009, greennewdealgroup.org. See also *The Cuts Won't Work*, greennewdealgroup.org.

Galbraith, J.K., *The Great Crash, 1929*, London: Penguin Books, 1992.

Geisst, Charles R., *Beggar Thy Neighbor: A History of Usury and Debt*, Philadelphia: University of Pennsylvania Press, 2013.

Graeber, David, *Debt: The First 5,000 Years*, New York: Melville House Publishing, 2011.

Guttmann, William and Patricia Meeham, *The Great Inflation*, Farnborough: Saxon House, 1975.

Hudson, Michael, *Super Imperialism: The Origin and Fundamentals of U.S. World Dominance* (Second Edition), London: Pluto Press, 2003.

Martin, Felix, *Money: The Unauthorised Biography*, London: The Bodley Head, 2013.

Murphy, Richard, *The Courageous State*, London: Searching Finance, 2011.

Smith, Yves, *ECONNED: How Unenlightened Self Interest Undermined Democracy and Corrupted Capitalism*, London: Palgrave Macmillan, 2010.